99 Activities and Greetings

Great for Morning Meeting... and other meetings, too!

Melissa Correa-Connolly

GRADES K-8

ISBN 1-892989-20-4

Library of Congress control number 2004113566

Cover and book design: Woodward Design

Northeast Foundation for Children
85 Avenue A, Suite 204
PO Box 718
Turners Falls, MA 01376-0718

800-360-6332

www.responsiveclassroom.org

09 08 07 06 05 04   9 8 7 6 5 4 3 2 1

Table of Contents

Acknowledgments

First and most important, I wish to thank all of the teachers who have welcomed me into their classrooms over the years and shared the many wonderful activities and greetings they do with children. It's because of you that this book exists.

I also wish to thank all of my colleagues at Northeast Foundation for Children who have made the *Responsive Classroom®* approach a regular and sustaining part of my life for so long. Special thanks to Chip Wood, who first introduced me to the *Responsive Classroom* approach.

And I thank my family who was and continues to be so patient and supportive of me while I try to do many things at once.

Many other people had a hand in making this book a reality. Specifically, they moved it from a raw manuscript to a beautiful and easy-to-use book. Thank you to:

- Allen Woods, editor, for bringing great clarity and order to the descriptions of the activities.

- Lynn Bechtel and Mary Beth Forton, project managers, for keeping the project moving along and for filling in the gaps whenever needed.

- Pam Porter and Adam Berkin, readers, for giving candid feedback that helped to make the book more useful for classroom teachers.

- Deborah Porter, reader, for sharing activities for primary grade students and for reading so carefully and thoughtfully.

- Alice Yang, for proofreading and for providing photographs of the illustrators.

- Leslie and Jeff Woodward, designers, for being enthusiastic about the project and bringing such care to the design.

- Roxann Kriete, director of NEFC, for supporting the project and for suggesting the idea of having children illustrate it.

- Dante, Ellie, Esther, Jessica, Kai, Martina, Sophia, Tess, Tyler, illustrators, for making the pages of this book so lively and beautiful. Thank you so much for sharing your artwork!

Activities

Name (page #)	Grade Level			Chant, Song, or Movements	Written Preparation or Special Materials	Early in the Year	Later in the Year	Can Be Used for Academic Review
	K–2	3–5	6–8					
Ali Baba (23)		X	X	X			X	
Around the World (24)		X	X		X		X	X
Bah Bah Boom! (26)		X	X				X	
Boog- A- Loo (27)	X	X	X	X			X	
Can You Guess? (11)		X	X		X	X		X
Chucki, Chucki (28)	X	X	X	X			X	
Clown Got Sick (30)	X	X					X	
Commonalities (12)	X	X	X		X	X		
Cookie Jar (31)	X	X		X			X	
Cups (32)			X	X	X		X	
Down by the Banks (34)		X	X	X			X	
Do You Want to Buy a Duck? (36)	X	X	X				X	
Earth, Air, Water, Fire (38)	X	X	X				X	X
Find Your Match (39)	X	X	X		X		X	X
Getting to Know You (14)	X	X	X		X	X		
Ghost Spelling (40)	X	X	X				X	X
Going to Kentucky (42)	X	X		X			X	
Ha, Ha (44)	X	X					X	
Hello Friend (45)	X			X			X	X
Hidey Ball (46)	X	X		X	X		X	
If I Were . . . (16)	X	X	X			X		X
I Have . . . Who Has? (47)		X	X		X		X	X
I Like Everything (48)	X	X	X				X	
Info Seek (49)	X	X	X		X		X	X
In Search of a Noun (50)		X	X				X	X
In the Way of the Adverb (51)		X	X				X	X
It Really Is . . . (52)	X	X	X				X	
It's My Job (53)	X	X		X			X	
I've Never . . . (17)	X	X	X			X		
Just Like Me (18)	X	X	X		X	X		
King or Queen Calls (54)	X	X	X		X		X	X
Letter (or Word) Search (56)	X				X		X	X
Listen to This (57)		X	X		X		X	X
Magic Number (58)		X	X				X	X

Name	Grade Level			Chant, Song, or Movements	Written Preparation or Special Materials	Early in the Year	Later in the Year	Can Be Used for Academic Review
	K–2	3–5	6–8					
Maître D' (59)	X	X	X		X		X	X
Match-Up (60)	X	X	X		X		X	X
Milling to Music (61)	X	X	X		X		X	X
Mrs. Marbles (62)	X	X					X	
Mystery Word (63)	X	X					X	X
Name Four (64)	X	X	X		X		X	
Name Ten (65)		X	X		X		X	X
No, No, No (66)	X	X	X				X	
On Fire (67)		X	X				X	
Ooh—Ahh (68)	X	X					X	
Partners and Pairs (69)	X	X	X				X	
Pass the Chicken (70)	X	X	X		X		X	X
Password (71)		X	X		X		X	X
Pebble, Pebble (72)	X	X	X	X	X		X	
Pedoodle (73)	X	X	X				X	X
Pros and Cons (74)		X	X				X	X
"Read All About It" Bingo (76)	X	X	X		X		X	X
Real Me (78)	X	X			X		X	
Secret Elf (19)	X			X		X		
Shoes (79)	X			X			X	
Silent Line-Up (80)	X	X			X		X	X
Sound of Things (81)	X	X					X	X
Syllable Choir (82)	X	X					X	X
Take Sides (20)	X	X	X		X	X		
Thing in the Bag (83)	X	X			X		X	
Three Clues (84)	X	X	X		X		X	X
Toe to Toe (85)	X			X			X	
Train (86)		X			X		X	X
UFO Experts (87)		X			X		X	
Wadlee Atcha (88)	X	X	X	X			X	
Watch It (90)			X		X		X	
When I Grow Up (91)	X						X	
When Pigs Fly (92)	X	X					X	
Where's My Chicken? (93)	X	X	X		X		X	
Woof (94)	X			X			X	
Word Ball (96)	X	X		X	X		X	X

Activities

Greetings

Name	Grade Level			Chant, Song, or Movements	Written Preparation or Special Materials	Early in the Year	Later in the Year	Can Be Used for Academic Review
	K–2	3–5	6–8					
Around the Circle Hello (109)	X	X	X				X	
Baseball Greeting (110)	X	X	X				X	
Bead Exchange (111)	X	X	X		X		X	
Calling All Friends (112)	X	X	X				X	X
Category Greeting (113)	X	X	X				X	
Chicka Boom (99)	X			X		X		
Choice Greeting (114)	X	X	X				X	
Did You Know…? (115)	X				X		X	X
Farmer Calls (116)	X				X		X	
Galaxy Greeting (117)	X	X					X	
Good Day! My Name Is…(100)	X	X	X		X	X		
Greeting A-Round (102)	X	X		X		X		
Greeting Braid (118)		X	X				X	
High Five/Ankle Shake (119)		X	X				X	
Hullabaloo Greeting (120)		X	X				X	
Jump In, Jump Out (122)	X			X			X	
Knock, Knock (103)	X	X		X		X		
Moving Name (123)	X	X					X	X
Name Game (104)		X	X		X	X		
Photo Greeting (106)	X				X	X		
Shoe Twister Greeting (124)	X	X					X	
Silent Signal Greeting (125)		X	X				X	
Snake Greeting (126)		X	X				X	
Squeeze (128)		X	X				X	
2–4–6–8 (129)		X	X	X			X	
Weekend Is Near (130)	X	X	X	X			X	
Welcome Chant (132)	X			X			X	
What's the News? (133)	X	X	X				X	X
What's Your Name? (107)	X	X				X		

Introduction

For many years, I've been collecting tried-and-true greetings and activities for Morning Meeting from K–8 classrooms across the country. I find these in classrooms, at workshops, in teacher rooms, and over dinner conversations. I jot them down in notebooks, on the back of envelopes, on odd scraps of paper, and on restaurant napkins.

I collect these activities because I believe so deeply in their value. Like Morning Meeting itself, the activities collected in this book offer students the opportunity to practice important academic and social skills in a playful way. This is a powerful combination as children often learn best when they're having fun.

In today's educational environment with so much focus on accountability, teachers often worry about "wasting time" on fun activities when there's so much curriculum to cover. Rest assured that the activities in this book not only create an environment that's conducive to learning, but they help children learn content and practice skills required by state standards.

In addition to the specific skills children practice while participating in these activities—skills such as spelling, counting, reading, and active listening—there are many general skills important to learning that children develop through these activities. These are:

- Risk taking
- Choice making
- Problem solving
- Self-control
- Active participation
- Assertion
- Cooperation

These are skills that serve children well during Morning Meeting and throughout the rest of the school day.

This book is meant to complement *The Morning Meeting Book* written by Roxann Kriete (NEFC 2002). In *The Morning Meeting Book*, you'll find a guide to doing all four components of daily Morning Meetings as well as directions for over 100 greetings and group activities. However, since for some readers *99 Activities and Greetings* will be a first taste of Morning Meeting, I offer some basic information about Morning Meeting and the role of greetings and group activities on the following pages. You'll also find guidelines for using these activities and greetings successfully.

Introduction

Introduction

Morning Meeting

Morning Meeting, a key component of the *Responsive Classroom* approach to teaching, is a powerful tool for building community and integrating the teaching of social and academic skills. Every day, for fifteen to thirty minutes first thing in the morning, teachers and students gather in a circle to greet one another, share news, practice academic and social skills, and prepare for the day ahead.

The meeting consists of four components done in the following order:

1. GREETING: Students greet each other by name. There are many greeting activities, including handshaking, singing, clapping, and greeting in different languages.

2. SHARING: Students share information about important events in their lives. Listeners offer empathic comments or ask clarifying questions.

3. GROUP ACTIVITY: All participate in a brief, lively activity that fosters group cohesion (for example, reciting a poem, dancing, singing, or playing a game that reinforces social and/or academic skills).

4. NEWS AND ANNOUNCEMENTS: Children read the news and announcements chart that their teacher has written. The chart often includes an interactive activity and focuses children on the work of the day ahead.

Role of Greeting and Group Activity

Greeting

Morning Meeting always begins with Greeting. In Greeting, each child is welcomed by name and practices welcoming others.

The goals of the Greeting component are:

1. To set a positive tone for the day

2. To provide a sense of recognition and belonging

3. To help children learn and use everyone's name

4. To let children practice hospitality

Although greetings might reinforce academic content or challenge the intellect, the primary learning is social. In Greeting, children not only learn and practice the basic elements of greeting each other in a friendly way, they also gain experience in reaching across gender, clique, and friendship lines.

Group Activity

Group Activity is the third component of Morning Meeting. The children have been sitting quietly and listening carefully during the second component, Sharing. Now it's time to be more active and join together in a short, lively activity that helps build community and allows everyone to contribute at his/her own level.

The goals of the Group Activity component are:

1. To build community culture by developing a class repertoire of songs, games, chants, and poems

2. To foster active and engaged participation

3. To heighten the class's sense of group identity

4. To have fun together while gaining competence in key social skills

5. To reinforce the learning of curriculum content

There is a wide range of activities available for this component of Morning Meeting. In addition to the activities described in this book and in *The Morning Meeting Book*, children could also sing a song together, act out a scene from a book, or recite a poem.

The important thing is to choose activities that are age appropriate and accommodate a range of skill levels. Some activities will have a clear focus on a particular academic skill; others will offer practice in general skills such as listening, following directions, and exercising self-control. All activities should be active, inclusive, and engaging for the entire group.

Keys to Success with Greeting and Group Activity

Successful Morning Meetings require careful structuring, teaching, and managing. This is particularly true for Greeting and Group Activity, where children are often moving around, taking risks, and in physical contact with one another. Following are guidelines that will help ensure productive Greetings and Group Activities:

1. *Work with the children to establish behavior guidelines for Morning Meeting.* Children need to know what's expected of them during Morning Meeting. How should they sit? When can they talk? When do they need to be quiet? How should they walk when they cross the circle to greet someone? Early in the year, work with students to set up behavior guidelines. "What do we need to do to make sure everyone has fun, feels safe, and feels included during Morning Meeting?" the teacher might ask. The teacher can then shape the children's ideas into a set of positively stated behavior guidelines that are posted in the Morning Meeting area. Including the children in this way helps them feel invested in following the guidelines throughout the year.

Guidelines often include things like:

- Listen to the person who's talking
- Look at the person who's talking
- Keep your body in control
- Raise your hand if you want to talk
- Respect everyone's efforts

2. *Talk with the children about how the guidelines apply to Greeting and Group Activity.* Because the guidelines consist of a few broad statements, an ongoing task for the children is thinking about how the guidelines apply to specific situations. For example, what does it mean to keep your body in control when you're mingling with other students in a greeting activity? What does it mean to respect everyone's efforts during group activities? Since children are concrete thinkers, it might help to ask questions like "What will it look like to keep your body in control during today's greeting?" or "What do we do if someone makes a mistake during Group Activity today?"

3. *Model and practice the behaviors needed to be successful with Greeting and Group Activity.* It's important not to assume that children will know how to shake hands respectfully, move across the circle safely, take turns, or respond appropriately when someone makes a mistake. Early in the year, model and practice the basic routines and behaviors necessary for making Greeting and Group Activity successful; throughout the year, review these routines as needed and model and practice any new routines required by more complex greetings and activities.

Behaviors to model for Greeting include:

- Shaking hands respectfully
- Making friendly and respectful eye contact
- Using a friendly, warm voice
- Moving around the room in a way that keeps yourself and others safe

Behaviors to model for Group Activity include:

- Using an appropriate voice level
- Maintaining self-control during active games
- Taking turns

- Responding supportively when a classmate makes a mistake
- Choosing partners in a respectful way

Modeling

Throughout this book, we refer to the technique of modeling. Generally, teachers use modeling when they want to introduce a behavior that needs to be done in a particular way. Following is a step-by-step example of modeling how to greet each other in a friendly way. The teacher's words are in italics.

Steps in the Modeling Process

- Describe the desired positive behavior.

  We said that in Morning Meeting we will take care of everyone and that means we need to greet each other in a friendly way.

- Collect ideas from students if you think they know the appropriate behavior.

  Who has an idea of what we might do to greet each other in a friendly way?

- A student or the teacher demonstrates the positive behavior.

  Watch while Samantha greets Isaac and see what she does.

- Ask students what specific actions, language, and voice tone they noticed in the demonstration.

  What did you notice about how Samantha greeted Isaac? What made it a friendly greeting?

- Ask for an additional student demonstration if you need to reinforce the positive behavior.

  Who else can show us a friendly greeting?

- Invite all students to practice the behavior and state your expectation that the behavior will continue.

  Now we know how to greet each other in a friendly way. We'll need to remember how we did this as we do our greetings in Morning Meetings this year.

Introduction

Introduction

4. *Keep greetings and activities simple at first.* Early in the year, when children are still learning basic classroom routines and getting to know each other, introduce easy-to-do and low-risk greetings and activities. For example, in the first weeks of school, children might easily say "hello" warmly and respectfully but not be comfortable with a greeting that requires touching, such as a handshake greeting. Likewise, children might be successful with an activity where they interview each other but may not have the self-control to do an activity that requires a lot of fast movement.

5. *Throughout the year, pay attention to children's developmental and learning needs when you choose greetings and activities.* As you make choices of what greetings and activities to use, it is important to keep in mind that not all groups of students develop social and academic skills at the same rate. A greeting or activity that's suitable for one group of children may not be appropriate for a wiggly or shy or young-for-their-age group. Observe the students, gauge their interests and skill development, and choose accordingly.

Some considerations in choosing activities are:

- What is the predominant developmental age of the children?
- How well do children work and play together?
- What level of risk is appropriate for the group?
- Does the class need energizing? Do they need help focusing?
- Are there academic skills the children need to practice?

Introducing a Greeting or Group Activity

The way you introduce a greeting or group activity has a big impact on children's success with it. Here are some steps you can take to ensure that children have a positive experience:

1. Gather and prepare all materials needed for the greeting or activity.

2. Think ahead of time about the academic and social skills required for the greeting or activity. Are there any skills that children need to learn or review?

3. For complex greetings and group activities, consider introducing the activity over several days. For example, for a chant that has many accompanying movements, teach just a couple of movements per day for a few days before going through the entire chant.

4. Explain the greeting or activity and then model skills that are new or need review. In activities where there are complex instructions, you might want to do a "pretend" round of the activity to make sure everyone understands before starting "for real."

5. Monitor the activity closely, being ready to reinforce positive behavior, remind children about the behavior guidelines when necessary, and redirect children who are off track.

6. If children are having a hard time with a greeting or activity, don't hesitate to interrupt the action and once again model certain routines or skills. If children continue to have problems, stop the activity and try again another day.

7. Brainstorm with the children various ways to take turns so that the same children aren't always first, last, or in the middle. Also brainstorm ways for children to know who has already been greeted or had a turn. Taking the time to work out these details will save time later and will allow children to have responsibility for taking care of each other.

Introduction

How to Use This Book

The book is divided into two sections: Activities and Greetings. Because timing is so important, I've also divided both the activities and greetings into two sections:

- Those to introduce early in the year: these are uncomplicated, easy to teach, and designed to help children learn more about each other.

- Those to introduce later in the year: these build on previously learned skills, are more complex, and require a higher degree of self-control and group cohesion.

In order to help you easily find a particular activity or greeting, there is an index in the front of the book. Keep in mind that many of the activities in this book have been invented by or modified by children and teachers who have then passed them along to others. As you read the selections, you might discover a way to adapt an activity to make it work better for your class. Or you might find some greetings that you think would work well as group activities and vice versa. Please modify, embellish, and experiment freely. Just remember to have fun and share any new versions of these activities with others. Enjoy!

Activities

Activities
to introduce early in the school year

Can You Guess?

Students select three facts most people don't know about them. Classmates try to guess who is being identified. This works well as a "getting to know you" activity early in the year. It can also be used later in the year to review academic content.

Skills practiced

Focusing attention; making inferences; reading and writing; can be used to review academic content

Materials needed

Index cards (one for each student)

Preparing students for success

- Review with the class types of personal information which are okay to share with everyone.

- Brainstorm types of facts to write, such as "I'm the oldest of 5 kids." "I love insects!" or "When I grow up, I want to be a writer."

How to do it

1. Distribute one index card to each student and tell students to write legibly one to three interesting facts about themselves on the card, without writing their names. The facts should be okay to share with everyone and include things that others might not know.

2. Collect the cards, shuffle them, and then pass one to each student. If a student gets his/her own card, s/he should return it to the stack and choose another one.

3. Students take turns around the circle reading their cards aloud and trying to guess which person is identified. They get two guesses. If the student isn't identified, the writer raises a hand and says, "That's me!"

4. At end of the activity, ask students to reflect on any connections they made during the activity (for example, students might notice there are several students who are the youngest in their families or love to sing or....).

Variations

- Teachers can give children lead-in phrases such as "When I grow up, I want to be . . ." or "In the summer, I love to . . ."

- Students can prepare cards ahead of time and bring them to the meeting.

- Teachers can use this activity to review academic content by writing facts or clues on the cards about the content to be reviewed (characters from a book or social studies unit, countries in the world, states, historical events, etc.). Students take turns reading the clues and guessing who or what is being identified. At any point a student can ask for help from others in making a guess.

Can You Guess?

Grades 3–8

Getting to Know You

Getting to Know You

Grades K–8

This activity begins with small groups working to find common and unique qualities and ends with students sharing this information with the class. It's a great activity for students to get to know one another and find out about each other's experiences, families, out-of-school activities, etc. Younger students (K–2) can do this activity later in the year once they're familiar with Venn diagrams.

Skills practiced

Oral language; developing questions; classifying information; comparing and contrasting; charting information on a Venn diagram

Materials needed

■ A Venn diagram on a large piece of oak tag for each group (see sample below). Hoola hoops can be used with younger students to make Venn diagrams on the floor that they can actually step into.

■ Colored markers suitable for writing

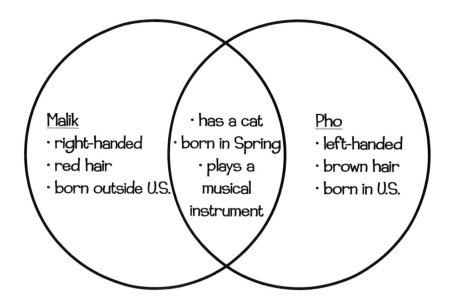

Preparing students for success

- Brainstorm possible questions students might ask in their small groups to find out things they have in common and things which make them unique. Questions can be about physical characteristics, out-of-school activities, family members, preferences, experiences, etc. Keep a list of the possible questions in a central place for students to refer to during the activity. The teacher can also prepare a list of questions or categories of questions ahead of time for students.

- Model for students how to frame their common and unique characteristics in the positive rather than the negative. That is, students should be defined by what they do and like (Kai plays piano or Kai likes dogs) rather than what they aren't or don't like (Kai doesn't play violin or Kai hates dogs).

How to do it

1. Divide students into teams of two to four children and give each group a large Venn diagram on oak tag and markers in different colors.

2. Specify a time limit (usually five minutes). Challenge the children to come up with things that *everyone* in the group has in common.

3. When the group finds something they all have in common, they write (or draw) this in the center in one color. When they find something that is unique to one person in the group, they write this under the person's name on one of the outer sections of the Venn diagram.

4. When the time is up, students return to the circle and share the things they found they had in common and the things which make them unique.

5. Reflect as a group on what students learned during this activity. By listening to each other's sharings, students will also get ideas for future questions for this activity.

Getting to Know You

Grades K–8

If I Were . . .

Students are asked to imagine themselves as something else (such as a book, country, ice cream flavor, animal, etc.) and then to choose a specific preference (for example, "If I were a country I'd be Jamaica." Or "If I were an ice cream flavor I'd be caramel fudge.") In a light-hearted way, students express individuality.

Skills practiced

Oral language; active listening; making respectful, appropriate comments; creative thinking; making connections; can be used to review academic content

Materials needed

None

Preparing students for success

- Tell the students what the topic statement will be (for example, "If I were an animal, I'd be a _____") and brainstorm possible choices for this topic.

- Discuss the importance of making respectful and relevant comments after a student has shared. Model how this will look and sound before beginning.

How to do it

1. Write the topic statement on a chart or board and give students a few minutes to think of their choice.

2. The first student turns to the next student in the circle and says, "If I were an animal, I would be _____."

3. The second student then makes a relevant and respectful one-sentence comment about what the student said before turning to the next student and saying, "If I were an animal, I would be _____."

Example:

Alex turns to Tanya and says, "If I were an animal, I would be a lion."

Tanya responds, "I like lions a lot!" Tanya turns to Olivia and says, "If I were an animal, I would be a dolphin."

Olivia responds, "Dolphins are cool swimmers."

4. Continue until everyone has had a chance to make a statement and offer a comment.

Variation

Choices for questions are unlimited and can cover a wide range of academic topics (If I were a state, an insect, a body of water, a historical figure, a character in a book, etc.) and include student-generated ideas.

I've Never . . .

Students choose something they've never done but would like to do. Then they search for others in the class who have not had the experience either. Students get to share something they dream about doing.

Skills practiced

Oral language; active listening; making connections; cooperation and turn-taking

Materials needed

None

Preparing students for success

- Brainstorm activities that students have never done, but would like to do. For example, I've never been outside my home state, I've never eaten seafood, I've never ridden on a train, I've never skied, I've never swum in the ocean, etc.

- Review how to move safely around the room.

- Model how to partner up when the chime rings (turn to face the person closest to you) and decide who will go first.

- Teach older children (grades 3–8) how to do "rock, paper, scissors" if they don't know how.

How to do it

1. Children stand in a circle, ready to mix and mingle.

2. When the teacher rings the chime, students begin to mill about the circle.

3. When the chime rings again, everyone freezes and finds the closest partner.

4. In grades 3–8, partners do one round of "rock, paper, scissors" (or use another quick way to decide who will go first). The winner makes the statement, "I've never _____, but someday I'd like to." In K–2 classrooms, the two students can simply decide who will go first.

5. If the student's partner hasn't had that experience either, the two stay together for one more round and the other person makes an "I've never…" statement in the next round. However, if one person in the pair has had the experience and the other hasn't, then the pair splits up after the first round.

6. Ring the chime again to begin the second round. Students who need a new partner find one and again do "rock, paper, scissors" or decide in another quick way who will go first. The winner makes the "I've never . . ." statement.

7. Keep the activity moving quickly and play for five or six rounds.

8. Take a minute or two to reflect on the activity. Ask students what they learned about each other and if there was anything that was surprising to them.

I've Never...

Grades K–8

Just Like Me!

Just Like Me!

Grades K–8

A leader asks the class questions about traits, preferences, activities, families, and other characteristics to show how much the group has in common. Students respond by standing up and together saying, "Just like me!"

Skills practiced

Active listening; making connections; categorizing

Materials needed

Prepare a list of things students might have in common, stated in first person sentences. For example, you might include preferences (I like egg rolls, My favorite season is fall, etc.); games or sports played (I like to play chess, soccer, basketball, etc.); out-of-school activities (I've acted in a play, I've marched in a parade, I've been to the dentist recently, I've cooked a meal for my family, etc.); experiences (I've broken a bone, I've seen a bear in the wild, etc.); or moods (I'm feeling tired, I'm feeling energetic, I'm feeling sad, etc.). You can also brainstorm a list of statements with the class.

Preparing students for success

- If necessary, discuss and model how to safely stand up and sit down in the circle.

- Do a practice round so students can try out standing up and saying "Just like me!" in unison.

How to do it

1. Students sit in a circle. The teacher or a leader calls out a statement such as "I have a cat" and everyone whom the statement applies to gets up and says together, "Just like me!" Students then sit down and wait for the next statement.

2. The activity continues through ten statements.

3. At the end, reflect with children about what they noticed they had in common. Also encourage children to have more discussions about things they have in common during recess or lunch.

Secret Elf

This is a fun activity for young children (although I've seen many older children eager to join in). It promotes careful listening and self-control as children try not to give away the identity of the "elf."

Skills practiced

Active listening; auditory discrimination; taking turns

Materials needed

None

Preparing students for success

Talk about what students might do to keep the identity of the elf a secret. Practice this once or twice before beginning.

How to do it

1. Students sit in a circle all facing one direction.

2. Place a chair for the "guesser" at least ten feet away from the group, facing in the opposite direction.

3. Choose a volunteer from the group to be the guesser. This child sits in the chair facing away from the group.

4. The teacher (or whole group) says, "Elf, elf, there's an elf on my shelf. My elf is . . . ." Students in the circle who would like to be the elf raise their hands.

5. The teacher silently chooses an elf by pointing to a student. That student then uses a disguised voice to say, "It is I."

6. The child in the chair turns around and has three tries to guess who the elf is. If the child doesn't guess correctly after three tries, the elf stands up to reveal his/her identity.

7. A new round begins with the elf now becoming the guesser (if s/he wishes).

Secret Elf

Grades K–2

Take Sides

Students physically "take a side" according to their individual preferences by moving to a side of the room designated by the leader. Students group and regroup themselves repeatedly.

Take Sides

Grades 1–8

Skills practiced

Active listening; making choices; making connections; identifying similarities and differences; following directions

Materials needed

Prepare a list of contrasting statements about student preferences. Here are just a few examples:

"I like to sleep late in the morning" and "I like to get up early"

"I like sweet foods" and "I like salty foods"

"I like to swim in lakes" and "I like to swim in pools"

"I eat meat" and "I'm a vegetarian"

"I like to move slowly" and "I like to move quickly"

"I like rainy days" and "I like sunny days"

"I like to be on stage" and "I like to be in the audience"

"I like to be with big groups" and "I like to be with one friend"

Preparing students for success

Review and practice moving calmly from one side of the circle to the other without bumping into anyone or anything.

How to do it

1. Students begin by standing in a line down the middle of the circle.

2. Explain that statements are limited to two choices and students need to make a choice based on what is closest to true for them. For example, it may be that both things are true to some degree, but students make a choice about which they prefer.

3. The teacher or leader calls out a pair of statements and indicates to which side students should move. For example, "If you like to listen to loud music, go to the right. If you like to listen to soft music, go to the left."

4. As soon as students have reached their sides and looked around to see who else is in the group, the leader calls out another pair of choices.

5. Continue through the list. Occasionally, the caller may say, "If neither is true for you, go to the middle."

6. The last statement can be, "If you are a student in Mrs. Johnson's (your name) class, sit in a circle."

Variation

Later in the year ask the students to brainstorm a list of contrasting statements to use for this activity.

Take Sides

Grades 1–8

Activities
to introduce later in the school year

Ali Baba

A chanting activity that uses a simple two-line chant combined with a series of gestures. Students need to pay attention to the leader and to their neighbor to the right to see what action might accompany the second line of the chant. As more motions are added and the activity becomes more complex, older children often enjoy the challenge of seeing how many actions they can manage.

Skills practiced

Following directions; coordination; concentration; rhythm

Materials needed

None

Preparing students for success

- Brainstorm motions and actions the leader can use along with the second line of the chant.

- Model and practice the activity slowly before beginning the real thing.

How to do it

1. Students sit in a circle where they can all see the leader and their neighbor on the right. Choose a leader who will control the actions for the first round.

2. The leader and the group will say the following chant over and over:

   Ali Baba and the forty thieves
   Camels, horses, you and me!

3. The leader begins by saying the chant and making a simple motion to go with it (such as hand clapping). The group joins in the chant and imitates the leader's motions.

4. After saying the chant once or twice, the leader changes to a different motion on the second line of the chant (such as snapping fingers or tapping knees).

5. While the group continues saying the chant and doing the original motion, the person to the leader's left changes to the leader's new motion. When the chant is said again, the next person changes to the new motion as the second line of the verse is said. This continues around the circle, one person at a time.

6. As the new motion is making its way around the circle, the leader changes the motion again. Again the neighbor to the left changes on the second line and each student in turn will change when the second line is said.

7. The group continues to say the chant together but there are many different motions making their way around the circle. As the group becomes better at changing at the right time, the leader can increase the speed of the chant and the pace at which the motion is changed.

Ali Baba

Grades 3–8

Around the World

This activity is designed to review content facts, especially those to be memorized. The teacher or leader asks a question to two students who each try to be the first to answer it correctly. The goal is for everyone to participate and review facts they need to know in a playful way. It's important to talk with students ahead of time about how to support one another and keep this activity from becoming competitive. If you have a competitive group, you might want to try "Bah Bah Boom!" before attempting this activity. It can help to make mistakes feel less significant.

Skills practiced

Cooperating; active listening; supporting everyone's effort; reviewing any type of content (especially facts that need to be memorized such as math computations)

Materials needed

Index cards with content questions (math computations, states and capitals, vocabulary definitions, etc.)

Preparing students for success

- Stress that the activity is meant to be non-competitive and that the goal is for everyone to review the content facts. Suggest that all students pay attention to every question and come up with answers inside their heads even when it's not their turn.

- Model the activity and practice it before beginning. Pay special attention to modeling how classmates can show their support for one another.

- Talk about the fact that some students will feel disappointed if they make a mistake and ask for ideas about what the student might do in this situation.

How to do it

1. Students sit in a circle. Choose a student to start. That student stands behind the person sitting to the left.

2. The teacher or a leader asks one question from a card to the student standing and the student sitting. Both try to answer the question correctly as quickly as possible.

3. The student who answers correctly first then moves to stand behind the next student in the circle. If the one who answers correctly is the standing student, that student simply moves to stand behind the student to the left. If the one who answers correctly is the sitting student, that student then stands behind the next student in the circle and the student standing returns to sit in his/her original spot.

4. This process continues until all the content is reviewed. If one student makes it all the way around the circle, that student takes a seat and a new student is chosen to start.

Variation

If the class is large, it may be best to divide the group into two circles and have a student leader read the cards to one circle. You can also try using rows of seats instead of a large circle.

Around the World

Grades 3–8

Bah Bah Boom!

Bah Bah Boom!

Grades 3–8

A fast-paced activity that requires students to know right and left as well as the names of their classmates. Because students will change places in the circle, they will need to keep up with the names of their new neighbors. Even making a mistake is fun!

Skills practiced

Learning names; cooperating; learning and practicing right and left; quick recall of facts

Materials needed

None

Preparing students for success

- With younger students, review "right" and "left."

- Tell students they'll always need to know the name of the person to their right and left. Model how to politely ask someone their name if you don't know it. If it's early in the year, go around the circle and have everyone say their name before beginning.

- Model what the leader will do.

How to do it

1. Students stand in a circle. Choose one student to be the leader and stand in the middle.

2. The leader points to any student in the circle and begins to say, "Right! Bah bah boom, boom, boom!" (The leader can say either "right" or "left.")

3. The student that was pointed at has to name the student to her right (or left, as directed) before the leader finishes saying "Bah bah boom, boom, boom!" If she is successful, she stays in her spot. If she doesn't finish until after the last "boom!" or makes a mistake, she becomes the new leader in the middle.

Variation

Instead of saying names, students state an item from a category that the leader names at the beginning of the activity (for example, states, vegetables, rivers, birds, etc.). To start the activity, the leader points to a student in the circle and says "Bah bah boom, boom, boom!" The student must name something from the stated category before the last "boom!"

Boog-A-Loo

Creative movements accompany this chant. For example, students might be asked to "do" a Frankenstein, a jelly fish, a rapper dance, or any other idea the students can imagine. A fun activity that gets everyone moving.

Skills practiced

Gross motor; creative expression; cooperation; rhythm; oral language

Materials needed

A chart with the words written on it

Preparing students for success

- Brainstorm, model, and practice a list of possible movements that the leader can call out. These might include "doing" a Frankenstein, a jelly fish, a rapper dance, a ballerina twirl, a football strut, a kangaroo hop, a snake in the grass, etc.

- Practice safely doing dance movements in the circle.

How to do it

1. Students stand in a circle. Choose a student to be the leader. The leader stands in the middle.

2. The leader begins the chant below, calling for creative movements in the sixth line.

   Leader: *He . . ey! Let me see you boog-a-loo!*

   Group: *What's that you say?*

   Leader: *I said, let me see you boog-a-loo!*

   Group: *What's that you say?*

   Leader: *I said, boog-a-loo, boog-a-loo!*
   Now let me see you jellyfish!
   (or other movement)

   Group does the movement (moving like a jellyfish) while saying: *I said ooh ahh, ooh ahh ahh! I said ooh ahh, ooh ahh ahh!*

3. The chant begins again with either the same leader or a new one with a different movement each round.

Boog-A-Loo

Grades K–6

Chucki, Chucki

Chucki, Chucki

Grades 1–6

A chanting hand game that originated in Alaska. As students get better at this, they'll enjoy the challenge of doing it faster and faster, testing their verbal fluency and physical coordination. You might want to try some other hand games as well. Students are often a great source of hand games. Ask them to bring their favorites and teach the class. Miss Mary Mack *by Joanna Cole and* Hand Clap! *by Sara Bernstein are also good resources.*

Skills practiced

Gross motor; cooperating with a partner; verbal fluency; remembering a sequence

Materials needed

A chart with the words written on it

Preparing students for success

- Introduce this activity slowly. Especially for younger students, begin by teaching and practicing the movements alone before adding the words.

- Emphasize and model safe movements and gentle hand and arm motions.

- Make sure there is an even number of participants.

How to do it

1. Students form inner and outer circles that face each other. Each student joins hands with the person opposite them—they will be partners for the entire activity.

2. Everyone says the chant below and does the accompanying hand-clap movements.

3. Repeat the chant and actions several times, increasing the speed each time.

Chucki, Chucki

Grades 1–6

Words	Actions
Chucki	Holding hands, inner player pushes right arm forward while outer player pulls left hand back. They then repeat the process (in rhythm to the chant) with the other arms.
Chucki	Repeat the actions above.
E-mak-o-chuk	Still holding hands, partners cross their arms, one pair over the other pair, and then cross them the opposite way.
Ta-le-o-chuk	Repeat the actions above.

The Clown Got Sick

The Clown Got Sick

Grades K–5

This is a great energizer for young students as well as a good memory exercise. One student invents a motion for the class to do; a second student adds a motion to the first; then a third student adds a third motion; and the sequence begins again.

Skills practiced

Gross motor; moving safely in a group; following directions; remembering a sequence

Materials needed

None

Preparing students for success

- Brainstorm different motions children can use for this activity. Emphasize and model safe motions for the classroom.

- Practice the words before starting. It might be helpful to write them on a chart as well.

How to do it

1. Standing in a circle, the class says together, "The clown got sick, the clown got sick!" The teacher responds, "How did the clown get sick?"

2. The first student says, "The clown got sick from doing this!" The student demonstrates a motion, such as rubbing her belly. The rest of the class imitates her.

3. The class now says, "The clown got sick, the clown got sick!" while continuing to do the motion. The teacher again responds, "How did the clown get sick?" and the second student in the circle says, "The clown got sick from doing this!" The second student then does the first child's motion and adds one of his own. For example, he rubs his belly and walks in place. The class then imitates the second child (doing both motions).

4. The class repeats the chant and a third child adds a third motion to the other two. For example, she rubs her belly, walks in place, and nods her head. The class imitates the third child while saying, "The clown got sick, the clown got sick!"

5. At this point the teacher responds, "Stop, everyone. That's how the clown got really sick!" and everyone stops.

6. The chant can begin again with three new students demonstrating new motions.

Variation

With older children, you can add more than three motions. It gets progressively harder to do and remember all the motions added by each child, a challenge older students typically enjoy.

Cookie Jar

An old favorite chant that challenges students to name everyone in the class. It helps students review names and challenges them to think about ways to ensure everyone gets named. I have found that students up to fourth and even fifth grade enjoy this chant.

Skills practiced

Oral language; following a pattern; reading; rhythm

Materials needed

A chart with the words written on it

Preparing students for success

Brainstorm ideas for keeping track of who has been named and who hasn't. In large groups, a student who has been named might sit down, hold up a hand, or use another signal. For some groups, you may want to specify a pattern for naming (the student on the right or left, girls name boys, etc.).

How to do it

1. Students sit or stand in a circle. Choose and identify the first student to be named. Remind everyone that the goal is to name everyone in the group.

2. The teacher or a leader begins the chant and the group names the first student. The first student names a second, the second names a third, etc., until all are named as in the following example:

Leader: *Who stole the cookie from the cookie jar?*

Group: *Amy stole the cookie from the cookie jar?*

Amy: *Who me?*

Group: *Yes, you!*

Amy: *Couldn't be!*

Group: *Then who?*

Amy: *Lara took the cookie from the cookie jar!*

Lara: *Who me?*

Group: *Yes, you!*

Lara: *Couldn't be!*

Group: *Then who?*

3. When the last person is named, the leader can say, "So that's who stole the cookie from the cookie jar!"

Variations

■ Students can invent other "crimes" that can be used in the chant instead of "stole the cookie from the cookie jar."

■ Young children can make a big book with this chant to help them with learning how to read names.

Cookie Jar

Grades K–5

Cups

Cups

Grades 6–8

An activity for older children that requires close attention to the directions of the leader, concentration, and teamwork. It is a great activity for indoor recess as well.

Skills practiced

Working as a team; gross motor; following directions; concentration; rhythm

Materials needed

- One plastic drinking cup for each student. Mark the bottom of one cup so it can be recognized.
- A chart with the words written on it

Preparing students for success

Teach the motions one at a time and practice until each motion is completed easily.

How to do it

1. Students sit cross-legged in a circle. Distribute one cup to each student. One student will receive the marked cup. Cups are placed with the open end down on the floor in front of the students.

2. The goal of this activity is to do the motions until the marked cup returns to its original place. Cups always are passed to the right (counter clockwise) and always are tapped with the right hand.

3. The leader demonstrates the motions while saying them out loud. Everyone performs the same motions at the same time. Students move the cup in front of them at the same time the leader says, "Pass."

4. All students now have a new cup in front of them. Repeat the motions until the marked cup returns to its original spot.

Variations

- Once children are comfortable with this version they can invent other motions to add or substitute.

- You can also increase the pace once students have mastered the motions. Challenge students to get the marked cup around the circle in a certain amount of time and then try to beat this time on another day.

Cups

Grades 6–8

Motions named by leader	What students do in response
Tap, tap	Tap cup on bottom twice with right hand.
Clap, clap	Clap hands twice.
Tap	Tap cup.
Pick up	Pick up cup.
Pass	Put cup halfway between you and person on right.
Clap, clap	Clap hands twice.
Pick up	Pick up same cup.
Bang, bang	Tap cup on floor twice and return cup to floor.
Clap	Clap hands.
Pick up	Pick up cup.
Pass	Place cup in front of person to right.

Down by the Banks

This chant activity requires students to send a gentle tap on the hand around the circle. The leader can choose to make the chant and the accompanying taps go quickly or slowly or a combination of the two. When the chant ends, the last student tapped becomes the new leader.

Skills practiced

Gross motor; cooperating; oral language; reading; rhythm

Materials needed

A chart with the words written on it

Preparing students for success

- Model and practice how to hold hands so the right hand is available for tapping and being tapped.

- Model and practice "gentle tapping" (palms up, right hand tapping the palm of the right hand of the neighbor to the left).

- Remind students that the goal of the activity is to have fun—there are no winners or losers.

How to do it

1. Students stand in a circle and hold their hands out, palms up.

2. Students move their left hand under the right hand of their neighbor to the left. Hands are positioned correctly when all students have their right hands above their neighbors' hands on the right and their left hands under their neighbors' hands on the left.

3. Choose a leader to begin the chant. The leader starts the chant while taking her right hand and gently tapping the upturned palm of her neighbor on the left. The leader decides if the chant will be said slowly, quickly, or using a combination of speeds.

Down by the banks
Of the Hanky Panky
A bull frog jumps
From bank to banky
Fe, Fi, Fo, Fum!
Watch how the bull frog
Jumps!

4. Students continue to pass the tap around the circle, one at a time during the chant.

5. When the last word of the chant is said ("Jumps!"), the person who would be the last person tapped tries to avoid it by pulling his hand back. If he is successful, and the tapper taps her own palm, then the tapper becomes the leader. If the last student doesn't pull his hand back quickly enough and is the last one tapped, he is the new leader. Students only get one turn as leader.

Variation

There are many versions of this chant. Children can be challenged to come up with a different chant, add a tune to this one, or add verses of their own.

Down by the Banks

Grades 3–8

Do You Want to Buy a Duck?

Do You Want to Buy a Duck?

Grades K–6

A fun activity where students need to repeat a pattern of words all the way around a circle. It works best with smaller groups (less than twenty). You can add variations to make it more difficult once students learn the easier version.

Skills practiced

Cooperating; listening carefully; following a pattern

Materials needed

None

Preparing students for success

Model the activity before beginning.

How to do it

1. Students sit in a circle. Choose a student to start.

2. The first student turns to his neighbor on the left and says, "Do you want to buy a duck?" The second student responds, "Does it quack?" and the first answers, "Yes, it quacks!"

3. The second student turns to her neighbor on the left and repeats the question, "Do you want to buy a duck?" Her neighbor asks the same question, "Does it quack?" Instead of answering, she turns to the first student and asks, "Does it quack?" The first student answers, "Yes, it quacks!" The second students turns to the third and says, "Yes, it quacks!"

4. The process continues around the circle with the "Does it quack?" question always passed around the circle to the first student, who is the only one who can answer "Yes, it quacks!" The "Yes, it quacks" response is then passed back around the circle to the current questioner.

5. When the last student hears that the duck does quack, she says, "I think I'll buy a duck!" and the activity ends.

Example:

Lenny, the first student, turns to his neighbor on the left, Maria, and says, "Do you want to buy a duck?"

Maria responds, "Does it quack?"

Lenny answers, "Yes, it quacks!"

Maria turns to her neighbor Alma and repeats the question, "Do you want to buy a duck?" Alma asks Maria, "Does it quack?" Maria turns back to Lenny and asks, "Does it quack?"

Lenny responds, "Yes, it quacks!" Maria turns to Alma and reports, "Yes, it quacks!"

Alma turns to her neighbor, Joel, and asks the same question, "Do you want to buy a duck?" and Joel responds by asking Alma, "Does it quack?" The question is repeated back around to Lenny, who is the only one who can answer, "Yes, it quacks." His answer is passed back to Joel and the process is repeated.

When the student to Lenny's right, George, gets the answer that the duck does quack, George ends the activity by saying, "I think I'll buy a duck!"

Variations

■ Once students can easily do this activity, time how long it takes to pass the question all the way around the circle and then try to beat that time.

■ Another "advanced" variation is to try passing two questions around the circle in opposite directions. For example, "Do you want to buy a duck?" and "Does it quack?" will be passing around the circle in one direction while "Do you want to buy a cow?" and "Does it moo?" is passed around the other direction. Both start at the same time and it's bound to get fairly silly somewhere in the middle.

Do You Want to Buy a Duck?

Grades K–6

Earth, Air, Water, Fire

Earth, Air, Water, Fire

Grades 2–8

A fun activity that helps children review kinds of animals and the environments where they live.

Skills practiced

Cooperating; vocabulary; building general knowledge about animals and environments where they live; categorizing; quickly recalling facts

Materials needed

The list of categories—earth, air, water, fire—written on the board or a chart (if necessary)

Preparing students for success

Brainstorm lists of possible animals beforehand.

How to do it

1. Students stand in a circle. Select one student to be the leader. This student stands in the middle of the circle to begin the activity.

2. The leader points to any student in the circle and calls out one of the categories (earth, air, water, fire).

3. If the leader calls out earth, air, or water, the student pointed at has to respond within three seconds by naming a specific creature that lives in that environment (not just "fish" or "bird," but "trout" or "cardinal"). If the student successfully answers, the leader moves to someone else in the circle and calls out another category.

4. Animals cannot be repeated. If the student can't name a new animal or repeats one, that student moves to the center to become the new leader.

5. If the leader calls out fire, the student pointed at becomes the new leader in the center. Students get only one chance to be in the middle. If they make a mistake a second time, they can choose a volunteer to be the new leader.

Variation

Use different categories (such as environments like the desert, ocean, and rainforest) and students can provide particular facts about the environment as a way to review content.

Find Your Match

Students mix and mingle to find the student holding a matching card. This is a good activity for reviewing academic content at all grade levels. When everyone has found his/her "match," pairs of students read their matching cards to the whole class. It is similar to the activity "I Have . . . Who Has?"

Skills practiced

Reviewing material from any content area (reading, language arts, vocabulary, poetry, social studies, etc.); reading; a variation can help with name recognition

Materials needed

Prepare pairs of cards which contain matching information in the chosen content area, with one card for each student. If there is an odd number of students, prepare one group of three cards. Examples of content include synonyms, antonyms, rhyming words, vocabulary words and definitions, contractions, states and capitals, math problems and answers, time tables and answers, social studies questions and answers, poems cut up into one or two line strips, etc. For younger students, you might use numerals and number words, colors and color words, capital and lower case letters, sight words and pictures, etc.

Preparing students for success

- If necessary, review expectations for moving safely around the room.
- Show several examples of matching cards and model what it will look like to approach someone to see if your cards match.

How to do it

1. Shuffle the cards and distribute one to each student.
2. Allow students to mix and mingle until they find their "match."
3. When everyone is paired up, you can review the content by asking each pair to report their matching information.

Variations

- You can combine a greeting and activity by having students first find the card that matches theirs. The two students then greet each other before they report their information to the class.
- To use just as a greeting, prepare one card with each student's name. Go around the circle and let each student draw a card. Each student, in turn, identifies the student on the card and greets that student appropriately (eye contact, strong and friendly voice, handshake or other gesture, etc.).

Find Your Match

Grades K–8

Ghost Spelling

Students work together to spell challenging words as a group. Students can refer to a word wall or other resource in the classroom. A variation allows younger children to play in a slightly different way.

Skills practiced

Cooperating; spelling; phonics

Materials needed

Chart or blackboard to use as visual aid

Preparing students for success

Model the activity before beginning and emphasize that students are working together to spell words. There are no winners or losers.

Ghost Spelling

Grades K–8

How to do it

1. The goal of the activity is to make words as a group, the longer the better. Each student around the circle contributes a letter in turn to build a word. Each student also tries to avoid completing a word. For example, if the letters that have been already said are "s-i-m-p-l," the next person will try to add a letter that can be built on (such as "i") rather than a letter that would complete the word (such as "e").

2. When a word is completed, a student writes a letter from the word "ghost" on the board. The activity ends when the word "ghost" is spelled out.

3. If a student can't think of a letter to add that would potentially make a real word, that student can challenge the previous student to say a word that incorporates the letters already given. Using the example in step 1, if six students have come up with "s-i-m-p-l-i" the seventh student could ask student number 6 to say a word using those letters. If student 6 comes up with a real word, such as "simplify," the activity begins again. If student 6 doesn't come up with a real word, then he writes a letter from "ghost" on the board.

Example:

Sonia is first. She says the letter "m."

Jay says "a."

Lia says "l."

Robbie could say "t" (malt), "l" (mall), "e" (male), etc. and complete a word, but he adds another letter to continue building a word. He chooses "i" (malice).

Steven, who goes next, doesn't know the word Robbie is spelling and challenges him. "Is this a real word?" If Robbie hadn't thought of a word such as "malice" but had just randomly chosen a letter, he puts the first letter of "ghost" on the board. If he does say a real word such as "malice," the activity continues with Robbie beginning a new word.

If Robbie had chosen to say "l" and complete the word "mall," it is up to the next student, Michelle, to try to add another letter (such as "e", malle__) that would make another word. If she can, the activity continues. If she can't, Robbie writes the first letter of "ghost" on the board. The activity continues until no letters can be added to the word.

Variation

For younger children, the object can be to complete the word. The class tries to make as many words as possible in a given amount of time. As words are finished, the teacher puts the word on the board to keep track of how many words the class makes and to reinforce the spelling skills practiced in this activity.

Ghost Spelling

Grades K–8

Going to Kentucky

In this simple activity that gets students moving, one student leads the rest in a chant with accompanying movements.

Skills practiced

Gross motor; following directions; rhythm and rhyming; reading

Materials needed

A chart with the words written on it

Preparing students for success

- Model safely holding hands in a circle and moving in one direction as a group.
- Model appropriate shaking and dancing.

How to do it

1. Choose one student as leader to stand in the center of the circle.

2. All students in the circle say the chant and make the movements that the chant directs.

3. At the end, the leader points to a student who then becomes the next leader.

Chant	Actions
We're going to Kentucky	Students hold hands and walk around in a circle while the leader stands in the center of the circle.
We're going to the fair *To see the senoritas* *With flowers in their hair*	Continue above.
Oh! Shake it, shake it, shake it!	Students stop walking and let go of hands. Students and leader begin to shake their bodies.
Shake it all you can! *Shake it like a milkshake* *And do the best you can*	Students continue shaking.
Oh! Rumble to the bottom	Students and leader wiggle down to a squat.
Rumble to the top	Students and leader wiggle back up.
Round and round and round we go *And where we stop, nobody knows*	Students in the circle stand still while the leader closes his eyes and turns around with his arm extended and finger pointing.
1,2,3,4, Stop!	Leader stops spinning at "Stop!" and points his finger at the person directly in front of him. That person becomes the new leader and it starts all over again.

Going to Kentucky

Grades K–5

Ha, Ha

A simple word, such as "Ha," is passed around the circle as quickly as possible. Because the activity is so silly, one goal can be to try to complete it without laughing!

Skills practiced

Following directions; paying attention; cooperating

Materials needed

None

Preparing students for success

- Practice pointing and passing the word before trying to go fast.

- Decide how students will tell if someone has received the word yet (students sit down after they receive it, hold up a hand, etc.).

Ha, Ha

Grades K–3

How to do it

1. Children stand in a circle. To pass the word, a child puts his or her hands together, points at another child in the circle, and says "Ha!" Each passer can choose to say "Ha!" once, twice, or three times, varying the rhythm and emphasis.

2. The first student points at someone across circle and says "Ha!" (or "Ha HA!" or "Ha, Ha, HA!"). The student who received it points at someone else and sends it on by repeating what the first student said and trying to keep the same rhythm and emphasis.

3. The activity continues until everyone has received a "Ha!"

4. The goal of the activity is to pass the word "Ha!" around the circle as quickly as possible.

Variations

- Other words can be used, such as "Boo!" "Burp!" "Ah-ah-choo!" or "Yeah!" Children may come up with other ideas and try them out.

- Older children can try saying the word in a high-pitched voice, a gruff voice, a sing-song voice, etc.

Hello Friend

A call-and-response chant that provides practice in math. Eventually, students can lead the group and decide what items to count. They can also decide whether to count by 1s, 2s, or another multiple.

Skills practiced

Counting; multiplication; oral language; reading

Materials needed

A chart with the words written on it

Preparing students for success

Brainstorm ideas for what to count and ways to count (1s, 2s, etc.) before beginning.

How to do it

1. The teacher can lead the chant or children can take turns leading once they learn it. The leader tells what to count, how to count, and how high to count. For example, the leader might decide to count marbles by 2s up until 20.

2. Each time the chant is said, you can change what to count, how to count, and how high to count. However, in the beginning, you may want to repeat it several times the same way until children learn the words.

Chant:

Leader: *Hello, hello, hello, friend! Can you come out to play, friend?*

Class: *No, friend!*

Leader: *Why, friend?*

Class: *I'm busy counting _____, friend!*

Leader: *How many can you count, friend?*

Class: *I can count to _____!*

Leader: *Let's count them all together, friend!*

Everyone, clapping with each number:
   1, 2, 3, 4...

Example:

Leader: *We're going to count bears, and we're going to count to thirty, counting by fives.*

Leader: *Hello, hello, hello, friend! Can you come out to play, friend?*

Class: *No, friend!*

Leader: *Why, friend?*

Class: *I'm busy counting bears, friend!*

Leader: *How many can you count, friend?*

Class: *I can count to 30!*

Leader: *Let's count them all together, friend!*

Everyone, clapping with each number:
   5, 10, 15, 20, 25, 30!

Hello Friend

Grades K–2

Hidey Ball

A guessing activity in which the leader tries to guess which student is hiding a soft ball or bean bag behind her back. Young students enjoy the physical activity and the challenge of hiding something without giving it away.

Skills practiced

Cooperating; gross motor; oral language; rhythm

Hidey Ball

Grades K–5

Materials needed

A soft ball or bean bag

Preparing students for success

- Model safe throwing and catching.

- Practice hiding something without giving it away.

- Discuss and decide what happens if more than one person catches the ball, if someone catches it and drops it, etc.

How to do it

1. Select one student to be the thrower. The thrower stands facing away from the other students, who are all scattered in the circle area.

2. The thrower holds the ball and recites the chant, throwing the ball gently up and over his head when he says the last line of the chant.

Watch it, watch it
Here it comes
Big ball, little ball
Fun for all!
Here it comes!

3. When a student catches the ball, she hides the ball behind her back. All the other students also put their hands behind their backs while they respond together.

Player, guesser
Hear the call
One of us has caught the ball!

4. The thrower turns around and makes three guesses about who has the ball. If he guesses correctly, he chooses a new thrower. If he doesn't, the student holding the ball is the new thrower.

I Have . . . Who Has?

Students review academic content by taking turns asking and answering questions. The teacher prepares index cards ahead of time using information the class is studying.

Skills practiced

Active listening; reviewing any content area such as vocabulary, parts of a sentence, capitals, time, money, etc.; reading

Materials needed

Prepare index cards with the statement "I have . . ." at the top and "Who has . . . " near the bottom, completing each with the content material to be covered. For example, if the class has been studying states and capitals, a card might read "I have New York" and "Who has Rhode Island?" The answer to the question is the name of the state's capital city. There need to be exactly enough cards for the number of students in the group. Each card must be different and the final card should ask for the "I have" information of the first card.

Preparing students for success

■ Discuss what students can do if they need help from classmates. Practice giving and asking for help before starting.

■ Discuss and model how to respond in a supportive way if someone makes a mistake.

How to do it

1. Give one card to each student. Choose a student to begin the activity; that student will also be the last to play.

2. The first student reads her card: "I have New York. Who has Rhode Island?" The student who has Rhode Island calls out the capital of Rhode Island ("Providence") and then reads his card, "I have Rhode Island. Who has Massachusetts?" The student who has Massachusetts calls out the capital of Massachusetts ("Boston") and then reads his card, "I have Massachusetts. Who has New Hampshire?"

3. The activity proceeds with students reading their cards and calling out their answers until it comes back to the first person.

4. At any point, students can turn to their neighbors to ask for help.

**I Have...
Who Has?**

Grades 3–8

I Like Everything

An interview activity where each student makes up an interview question. Students enjoy mixing and mingling and performing a quick "interview." Questions may require just a one-word answer. Older children can keep a written record of their findings while younger children can report their findings orally. The activity moves quickly and can be different every time.

Skills practiced

Asking questions; responding to inquiries; using and understanding different nouns and verbs; remembering information; oral language

Materials needed

None

Preparing students for success

- Review how to move safely and calmly around the room.

- If necessary, review procedures for finding a partner and listening actively.

- Select a type of question to use. Types of questions can include: "Do you like… (ice cream, baseball, dancing, etc.)?" "Can you . . . (knit, sew, fix a pencil sharpener, stand on your head, etc.)?" "What's your favorite . . . (sport, dessert, band, subject in school, etc.)?"

- Brainstorm nouns or verbs that students can use to complete the question stem.

- Model an interview before beginning.

How to do it

1. Students begin by standing in a circle. Tell them the type of question stem they will be using and ask them to think of a noun or verb to complete it. Encourage them to be creative since the activity is more fun if everyone is using different questions.

2. When everyone is ready, use a chime to signal that they should find their first partner. Both partners ask the question they have decided on and listen carefully to the answers.

3. When partners have completed one "interview," they move to find another partner and ask the same question. Repeat the process until students have interviewed four or five partners. Use a chime to signal the end.

4. Children return to sit in a circle. Ask for volunteers to share some of the information they gathered.

Variation

Older students can keep track of responses to their question on a note card or pad. Later, they can use the information for graphs, reports, etc.

Info Seek

A versatile activity that teachers can use to build group cohesion or to review academic content. Students mingle, ask questions that have simple answers, and record this information on a survey sheet.

Skills practiced

Interviewing; reviewing any content area such as vocabulary, social studies, or science (especially memorized material); recording information; sharing information in a concise way

Materials needed

- Prepared "survey" or information sheets. The teacher and/or students can prepare a survey sheet with the questions that all students will use. Questions can be "getting to know you" type questions (find a person that has older brothers, was born in the summer, has two pets, walks to school, etc.) or questions about material from an academic unit (name a part of speech, name an animal that lives in the desert, name a food that has carbohydrates, name a river in the United States, etc.). Limit the survey to, at most, ten questions, fewer for younger students. Answers should be a single word or a short sentence since students need to gather information quickly.

- Clipboards and pencils

Preparing students for success

- Read the survey sheet aloud with the whole group before the interviewing begins, making sure the questions are easy for everyone to read.

- Model and practice how to ask and answer questions in a friendly way.

How to do it

1. Pass out one survey sheet, a clipboard, and a pencil to each student. Children mingle about the room collecting answers from classmates. They should get an answer to just one question from each person they "interview" and then move on to another classmate.

2. When you ring a chime, the group comes together to share the information. Read one question at a time and ask for a few volunteers to share what they wrote on their survey form.

Variations

- Students can create survey sheets during academic work periods to use the next day in Morning Meeting.

- Younger students can use illustrations or stickers to represent an interview question and checkmarks to record "yes" or "no" answers.

Info Seek

Grades K–8

In Search of a Noun

In this activity, one student asks other students in the group questions to try to identify a noun chosen by the group.

Skills practiced

Identifying and understanding nouns; identifying categories; developing questions; deductive reasoning

In Search of a Noun

Grades 3–6

Materials needed

None

Preparing students for success

Brainstorm questions for different categories of nouns (person, place, and thing) so children have some ready ideas when the activity begins.

How to do it

1. Students sit in a circle and one student leaves. The group decides on a noun (person, place, or thing). No proper nouns are used.

2. The student returns and is told whether the secret noun is a person, place, or thing.

3. The student tries to guess the secret word by asking three questions. Each question should begin with "who," "when," "where," or "why." For example, if the noun is a thing (a book, for instance), the questions might be "When might you use this?" "Why do you use it?" "Who uses this thing?" After each question, students who want to answer raise their hands and the student in the center calls on one person to answer each question.

4. After hearing the answers, the student gets two chances to guess the word. If the student doesn't get the word right, she calls on someone in the group to say the noun.

5. The activity then continues with another student leaving the circle.

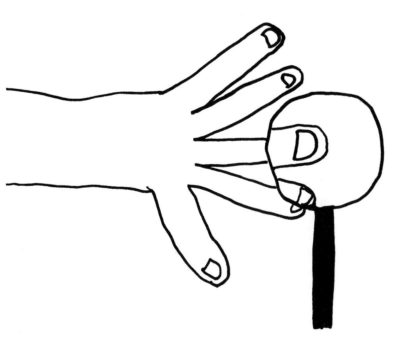

In the Way of the Adverb

This language activity uses pantomime to illustrate different adverbs. Students should be familiar with pantomime and quite comfortable with each other before doing this activity. The list of adverbs can be as creative and complex as the group can handle.

Skills practiced

Gross motor; reviewing and understanding the role of adverbs; vocabulary

Materials needed

None

Preparing students for success

■ Brainstorm with students a list of actions (reading, walking, sleeping, dancing, writing, etc.) and a list of adverbs that describe how these actions are done (happily, angrily, quickly, slowly, etc.). Post both lists on the board or a chart.

■ Model and practice how to pantomime some of the actions (dancing) and then combine the actions with the adverbs (dancing slowly) before beginning.

How to do it

1. Students sit in a circle. Choose one to be the guesser and have the guesser leave the circle to a place where she can't hear what's said in the group.

2. Students in the circle select an action and an adverb (such as "reading quickly").

3. The guesser comes back to the middle and is told what the action is ("reading") but not the adverb. The guesser then calls on a student for a clue.

4. The student pantomimes the action and adverb (leafing through a book very quickly, as if speed reading). The guesser can guess an adverb from the list right away or get as many as two more clues from other students before guessing.

5. The teacher tells the student whether it's the right adverb or not and chooses another guesser.

In the Way of the Adverb

Grades 3–6

It Really Is . . .

Children use their imagination to describe some possible uses for a common object. They then use their dramatic skills to pantomime how the object might be used.

Skills practiced

Oral language; creative expression

Materials needed

Any common object or material from the classroom—a pen, piece of paper, book, chair, lunch box, glue, etc.

Preparing students for success

- Brainstorm possible uses of the object so students feel safe in choosing creative uses for it.

- Model how it will look to pantomime a possible use for the object.

- Let students know that they can pass when the object comes to them.

It Really Is . . .

Grades 2–6

How to do it

1. Select an item from the room, such as a pen, and pass it around the circle.

2. The first student begins by saying: "This looks like a pen, but it really is . . . a baton!" and pantomimes using a baton. The object is passed to the next student.

3. The next student takes the object (a pen) and says, "This looks like a baton, but it really is a . . . walking stick!" and pantomimes using a walking stick.

4. The activity continues around the circle until it returns to the first student and each person has had a chance to describe and pantomime a new vision of how to use the object.

Variation

Students can pantomime the use of the object without naming it. The group tries to guess the use before moving on.

It's My Job

One student pantomimes doing a particular job; other students guess what the job is. Students should be comfortable with each other and have some experience in charades or other pantomime activities. It is similar to "When I Grow Up" but is slightly more complex.

Skills practiced

Learning about different occupations; vocabulary; observing carefully; oral language; reading

Materials needed

A chart with the words written on it

Preparing students for success

- Brainstorm a list of jobs (mechanic, hairdresser, police officer, airplane pilot, firefighter, etc.) and how they can be acted out.

- Practice pantomime and encourage students to exaggerate their actions so people understand what they are doing.

- Practice the call and response.

How to do it

1. Students sit in a circle. Choose one student to be the leader and stand in the middle. The leader chooses a job to act out but doesn't tell the group.

2. The leader and the group use a call and response to say the following chant.

Group: *Hey friend, where'd you come from?*

Leader: *The busy people's station!*

Group: *What's your occupation?*

Leader: *Almost anything!*

Group: *Then get to work!*

3. At the end of the chant, the leader acts out the occupation and the group tries to guess what it is. When someone guesses correctly, a new student becomes the leader.

It's My Job

Grades K–3

The King or Queen Calls

This activity combines movement around the room (similar to Musical Chairs) with identifying categories and the things that fit in them. It's a fun way to review academic content but it's best done later in the year when teachers are sure students know the basic routines and can use self-control.

The King or Queen Calls

Grades K–8

Skills practiced

Categorizing; reviewing any type of academic content (social studies facts, geography facts, number facts, prefixes/suffixes, etc.); reading

Materials needed

- Prepare two sets of index cards. The cards in one set, which the King or Queen draws from, will name categories (for example, for a review of math facts the categories might be odd numbers, even numbers, prime numbers, multiple of 5, etc.). The cards in the other set, which will be distributed to each child, will name items in the categories (for example, for the math categories the items would include numbers such as 3, 12, 7, 25, etc.). For younger students you can use simple words (words starting with t, for instance) or even pictures or stickers.

- A circle of chairs in the meeting area

Preparing students for success

- Model moving safely around the chairs.

- Discuss and practice what to do if two students go to the same chair at the same time.

How to do it

1. Select one student to be the first King or Queen. This person stands in the middle of the circle. Remove this student's chair from the circle.

2. Distribute the item cards, one to each student seated in the circle.

3. The King or Queen picks a category card and calls out the information from the card. Any students with an item that fits in that category must get up and switch seats. The King or Queen also tries to find a seat.

Example:

The category on the King/Queen's card is "either prefixes or suffixes." Students each have a card naming a word that might have a suffix or a prefix. The King or Queen looks at the category card and calls out, "prefix." All students who have a word with a prefix must get up and move to another seat.

4. One student will be left without a seat when the change happens and that student becomes the new King or Queen. The former King or Queen takes the card from that student to play the next round. The new King or Queen draws a new category card and the process continues.

5. Students only get one chance to be King or Queen. If the King or Queen is left without a seat, then he or she chooses someone else to be the next King or Queen.

6. Review the content after each round or at the end of the activity to reinforce the learning.

The King or Queen Calls

Grades K–8

Letter (or Word) Search

Letter (or Word) Search

Grades K–2

This is a simple activity that is great for children just learning the alphabet. It can be easily adapted to practice early reading skills, such as learning sight words or beginning sounds. It is also a good activity for teaching students how to be helpful to classmates in academic areas. Try teaching it during language arts and then moving it to Morning Meeting for practice.

Skills practiced

Letter or word recognition; visual discrimination; cooperating; taking turns

Materials needed

- A highlighter
- Morning message or some other familiar passage written on a chart
- Letters or words written on index cards, one for each child in the group

Preparing students for success

- Acknowledge that every student will probably want a turn in this fun activity; explain how this will happen.
- Talk about and model ways that students can be helpful if someone gets stuck and can't find the letter (or word). Talk about why blurting out the answer is not helpful and establish that it will be up to the child who needs help to ask for it. Also, elicit ideas from the students about ways to give hints without giving away the answer.

How to do it

1. Students sit in a circle with the morning message or other chart placed so everyone can see it.

2. Explain to the students that they will be detectives trying to find letters or words on the chart.

3. Place the letter or word cards face down on the floor in the middle of the circle.

4. Each child takes a turn by choosing a card on the rug and finding the letter/word on the chart. The child says the letter/word aloud (or asks for a volunteer to help) and highlights it on the chart.

5. When a child is finished, s/he passes the highlighter to the next person in the circle.

6. When everyone has had a turn, ask students to reflect on what was challenging and how they helped each other.

Listen to This

Students learn or review content information using index cards prepared ahead of time by the teacher or students. Students frequently change partners and are required to listen closely to what someone else has to say.

Skills practiced

Oral language; active listening; learning or reviewing information in any content area

Materials needed

One index card for each student, each prepared with one interesting fact about something the class is studying. The teacher or the students can prepare these cards. The cards might include an important fact about one of the states; an interesting fact about the Civil War; one fact about the skeletal system; one vocabulary word and definition; a fact about the pyramids, etc.

Preparing students for success

- Review how to move safely and calmly around the room.

- Elicit from children and model the procedures for finding partners and for active listening.

- If necessary, teach children how to do "rock, paper, scissors."

- Make sure there is an even number of participants.

How to do it

1. Distribute one card to each student; students read the information silently. When you ring a chime, they get up and find a partner.

2. Partners do "rock, paper, scissors" to see who goes first. The first student shares the information on the card by reading it, followed by the other partner. When both are finished, they exchange cards.

3. Students then find a new partner and repeat the process with the new information. Ring a chime after about five minutes to signal students to return to their seats.

4. Ask for volunteers to name the most interesting fact they heard. You can also ask students to go around the circle and read the card they ended up with.

Listen to This

Grades 3–6

Magic Number

Magic Number

Grades 3–8

This activity offers practice in counting. By counting out loud and saying the "magic number" that students have selected, students move from one group to another and back.

Skills practiced

Cooperating; counting; multiplication

Materials needed

None

Preparing students for success

- Review how to move safely around the room.

- Discuss how students in the inside circle will let newcomers know their "magic number."

How to do it

1. Students begin by standing in a circle. Establish the counting pattern (by 1s, 2s, 5s, etc.). Ask for a volunteer to select and say out loud a first "magic number"—for example, 13 (be sure the number fits the counting pattern).

2. Starting anywhere in the circle, students count off, using the established pattern. The student who reaches the "magic number" says "magic" and goes to the center of the circle.

3. The student in the middle now chooses two other students to come into the center of the circle and selects a second magic number—for example, 7. This number is now the designated "magic number" for the inner circle.

4. The center group now begins counting, one at a time, while the outside circle also begins counting.

5. When a student in the outside circle says his group's magic number (13), he calls out "magic" and joins the inside circle, standing in any spot. When a student in the center circle says her group's magic number (7), the student calls out "magic" and joins the outside circle. Students move back and forth between circles regularly. No one is ever out or loses.

6. The group in the center chooses a different number each time they begin a new counting sequence. The most recent newcomer selects the number. The outside circle's number always stays the same.

7. The activity ends when a predetermined number of students are in the center group, or when the activity has lasted for five minutes.

Variation

Allow students to count up to three numbers on each turn. For example, the first student says, "1, 2" and the next says, "3, 4, 5."

Maître D'

Students form groups based on a number called out by the teacher or "maître d'." Once in the groups, the students take turns briefly answering a question called out by the teacher. The activity moves quickly and students frequently change groups. The questions that students answer can help students get to know each other or review content or recent events.

Skills practiced

Cooperating; following directions; using number sense; active listening; oral language

Materials needed

- A towel or cloth to drape on your arm like a maître d' in a restaurant

- Prepare a list of questions for small groups to discuss for a few moments. They might be "getting to know you" questions ("How many people in your family?") or questions related to content or recent activities such as a field trip ("Name something you saw on our field trip." "Name one interesting fact you learned on our field trip.").

Preparing students for success

Model and practice safe movements from group to group.

How to do it

1. Students begin by standing in the meeting area. You pretend to be a maître d' with a cloth draped over one arm.

2. Call out, "Table for four!" (or any other number from one to five depending on the number of students in the group). Students quickly form groups of that number, putting out a hand in the center to help define the group. Any students left over form a smaller group. (Be sure there is never one student left alone.)

3. When students are in groups, ask a question that each person will answer.

4. Then call out a new number and children form new groups. Ask a new question for children to answer.

5. Keep the activity moving quickly so that students get to be part of several groups.

6. At the end of the activity, ask for brief reports about what the children discussed.

Maître D'

Grades K–6

Match-Up

Match-Up

Grades 1–8

An activity in which students practice sequencing and review academic content. For example, students are given one line of a poem or song, an event on a timeline, a letter in the alphabet, a number, a stage of a life cycle in biology, or other segment of an ordered group. Students then get together with others who share parts of the same whole and work together to put the information in its proper sequence.

Skills practiced

Cooperating; sequencing; oral language; reviewing any type of sequenced content; reading

Materials needed

Copies of songs, poems, events in a historical timeline, stages in a life cycle, or other sequenced content. Cut into strips so that each student gets one strip.

Preparing students for success

- Review expectations for small group cooperation so that everyone is involved.

- Model how to help students out if they're uncertain about the information on their strip.

How to do it

1. Students sit in a circle. Distribute the prepared strips, one for each student.

2. Choose one student to begin. That student reads the information on the strip. Other children who share the same category of information identify themselves and form a group to one side.

3. Choose another student who repeats the process. Continue the process until all children are grouped.

4. Each small group works to arrange the strips in the correct order. The teacher moves from group to group, helping students determine the correct order if needed. Once the order is figured out, one person from each group (or the small group all together) reads the information aloud, presenting the content in its proper sequence.

Milling to Music

Students mill about the circle, moving to music, until the music stops. Students then partner up and ask each other questions, either as a way to review academic content or as a way to get to know each other.

Skills practiced

Cooperating; reviewing any content area; active listening; reading; oral language

Materials needed

- Tape or CD player and music to play on it

- Index cards with questions, one for each student. The questions can be about academic content (What's 5 x 5?) or about each other's interests, hobbies, preferences, etc. (What's one thing you like to do on the weekends?). For younger students (K–1), the question can be represented by a picture or be told to students verbally.

Preparing students for success

- Discuss and practice how to dance and move about safely in the circle when the music is playing.

- Model and practice finding a partner: turn to the person closest to you when the music stops and try to get a new partner each time.

How to do it

1. Give each student a card with a question written on it (when reviewing academic content, the answers can be written on the back of the card).

2. Play music for about 30 seconds while students mill about and dance. When you stop the music, everyone finds a partner who is nearby.

3. Children take turns asking and responding to questions on the cards.

Variation

Try using this activity to practice listening skills. Children find a partner and the teacher announces an open-ended question to the whole group. One person in each pair responds in a few sentences. The other person then paraphrases what was said.

Milling to Music

Grades K–8

Mrs. Marbles

Students have a lot of fun with this activity. The goal is to pass a simple message around the circle without showing their teeth. A nice tension-relieving activity.

Skills practiced

Cooperating

Mrs. Marbles

Grades K–5

Materials needed

None

Preparing students for success

Model the activity before beginning. Emphasize that there are no winners or losers and that the goal is to try to pass the message without laughing or smiling.

How to do it

1. Students sit in a circle. Before beginning, explain that students must ask and answer a question without showing their teeth, which means without smiling or laughing.

2. The first student says to the person on the left, "Hi! Have you seen Mrs. Marbles?" The second student responds, "No, I haven't, but I'll ask my neighbor!" The process is repeated around the circle.

3. When someone smiles or laughs, the questioning stops briefly and then begins again with the student who laughed.

4. The activity continues until students go completely around the circle without anyone laughing or smiling or until the allotted time is up.

Variation

One student is "it" and stands in the center. That student approaches each student in turn and asks, "Hi! Have you seen Mrs. Marbles?" and each responds, "No, I haven't, but you could ask my neighbor." If the seated student smiles or laughs, that student becomes "it" and moves to the center.

Mystery Word

Students try to figure out a mystery word by guessing individual letters. It's a great activity for building vocabulary and spelling skills and students rarely tire of it. Many teachers incorporate it into the News and Announcements portion of Morning Meeting.

Skills practiced

Spelling; word recognition; vocabulary

Materials needed

A chart to write the mystery word on

Preparing students for success

- Establish how many correct letters need to be in place before students can begin to guess the whole word.

- Practice giving clues that will give hints to the guessers without giving the word away.

How to do it

1. The teacher or a leader chooses a mystery word and places blank spaces representing the letters on a chart or board. For example, the mystery word might be "thunder" so the chart would read: __ __ __ __ __ __ __. Leaders can use sight words, words from a word wall or vocabulary list, or words related to particular themes (weather, science or social studies unit, literature, etc.).

2. Students in the class raise their hands to take turns guessing letters that might be in the word.

3. If a correct letter is guessed, the leader writes the letter in one of the blanks. If an incorrect letter is guessed, the leader writes it on the board or chart to serve as a visual reminder of the letters that have been guessed.

4. At any time, the leader can give out one or more clues to the class to help them figure out the word. For example, "It has something to do with our new theme."

5. After a few letters have been identified (two or three for shorter words, four or five for longer words), the leader can ask for guesses of the entire word.

Mystery Word

Grades K–5

Name Four

Name Four

Grades K–8

Students choose four categories from a list and think about favorite items within each category. They then mingle and share information with four different partners. The activity builds personal communication skills and helps students learn about each other.

Skills practiced

Sharing information verbally; active listening; following directions

Materials needed

Note paper so students can make notes on chosen categories and items in them (as needed)

Preparing students for success

- Review moving safely around the room.
- Review the procedures for finding a partner and active listening.
- Brainstorm in advance a list of categories for a particular letter and post the list where it can be seen. For example, categories for the letter "C" might include the following:

  cuisine (names of foods, food types, etc.)

  characters (from TV shows, from a book or movie, etc.)

  cookies

  colors

  cars (brands, kinds)

  cartoons

  cards (card games, trading cards, etc.)

How to do it

1. Students sit in a circle. Review the categories listed and clarify what type of items might belong in them. For example, "cards" might mean card games or kinds of greeting cards.

2. Each student decides on four categories (one or two categories for younger students) and chooses a single item for each category. Students select items that they have a personal connection to (a favorite color or a favorite card game, for instance).

3. When everyone is ready, students mix and mingle to find a partner. Both share the item from one of the categories they've chosen and why they chose that item.

4. When the first set of partners is done, call out "Switch!" The process is repeated three more times with students using a different category each time. After they have shared with four partners, ring a chime for students to return to the circle.

5. Ask volunteers to share something they learned about one of their classmates in this activity.

Name Ten

In small groups, students come up with a list of ten things they all have in common. Then they narrow the list down to a designated number and report back to the class. This is a good activity for team building. A variation can be used to review academic content.

Skills practiced

Cooperating; active listening; decision-making; a variation can be used for reviewing facts from any academic unit

Materials needed

One piece of paper and one pencil for each team

Preparing students for success

- Discuss, model, and practice the skills needed to be a good group member—careful listening, offering ideas respectfully, making decisions cooperatively.

- Brainstorm a list of not-so-obvious things that people could have in common with each other (for example, month or season of birth, being the oldest or youngest in family, having same number of siblings, hobbies, etc.). Rule out some very obvious choices (grade, age, class, etc.). Post the list so children can refer to it as they do the activity.

How to do it

1. Form several small teams. This works best if there are no more than four students on a team. In a small class, there might be only two students per team. Give each team a piece of paper and a pencil.

2. Each team designates one student to be the "recorder."

3. The teacher serves as the time-keeper. Each team has two minutes to find ten things they have in common that are not immediately obvious.

4. As each team comes up with an idea that works, they call out the number of the idea. This lets the teacher know how quickly teams are building their list. (Most teams are done before two minutes are called.)

5. When all teams have finished, give them one minute to decide on three things from their list that they want to share with the whole class.

6. Teams take turns sharing. If there's time, students can share other things they learned about each other, and what was hard or easy about the task.

Variation

Teams can come up with a list of facts they learned from a unit of study. The teacher designates the number of facts.

Name Ten

Grades 3–8

No, No, No

Students change one part of a sentence at a time until it is nothing like the way it started. This activity is a great way to practice oral language skills and encourage creative thinking. The original sentence can be shorter and simpler for younger students and more complex for older students.

No, No, No
Grades 1–8

Skills practiced

Active listening; sentence construction; creative thinking; oral language; following directions

Materials needed

A chart with the original sentence written on it

Preparing students for success

Model how to be supportive if a student gets confused and changes more than one part of the sentence (that is bound to happen).

How to do it

1. Create a sentence that contains several parts, such as who, what, when, where, and with whom. For example: "Yesterday, my friend Jane and I went to the library and we saw the biggest dictionary we had ever seen!"

2. Students take turns repeating the sentence, but each student changes one thing, in turn. Students need to include the changes that have preceded theirs.

3. For example, the first student might say, "No, No, No! Yesterday, my friend Adam and I went to the library and we saw the biggest dictionary we had ever seen!"

4. The next child in turn might say, "No, No, No! Last week, my friend Adam and I went to the library and we saw the biggest dictionary we had ever seen!"

5. The next child might say, "No, No, No! Last week, my friend Adam and I went to the mall and we saw the biggest dictionary we had ever seen!"

6. The children continue changing the sentence as it goes around the circle until it returns to you. When you hear the last version, you can say, "Oh, so that's what happened!"

On Fire

This activity is derived from a popular African game. The leader gives students a "magic word." Students then need to use their best listening and remembering skills to determine whether they should stand up or stay seated when the leader calls out a sentence that might—or might not—contain the magic word.

Skills practiced

Active listening; memory

Materials needed

None

Preparing students for success

- Model the activity with a few student volunteers before beginning the real thing. Many students will need to see what this one looks like first before participating.

- Let students know that the leader will always be the one to decide who stands up last. This will often be a close call and it's important that students don't argue with the leader's decision. Emphasize that there are no winners or losers in this activity.

How to do it

1. Students sit in circle. Choose one student to start in the middle as a leader.

2. The leader chooses one of three words (mountains, river, or forest) to be the "magic word" and tells the group.

3. The leader then walks around the circle and calls out one of the following sentences:

Fire in the mountains!

Fire in the river!

Fire in the forest!

4. The leader can call out the sentences in any order. If the magic word is not in the sentence, the students in the circle call out "Fire!" If the magic word is in the sentence, students stand up as soon as they hear the word.

5. When the leader uses the magic word, the last person who stands up becomes the new leader. If a student stands up before the leader uses the magic word, that student becomes the next leader.

On Fire

Grades 2–6

Ooh—Ahh

Ooh—Ahh

Grades K–5

A simple activity where students hold hands and pass a gentle squeeze around the circle. When sounds are added to the squeeze, the direction of the squeeze can change quickly. Students need to be alert.

Skills practiced

Gross motor; paying attention; cooperating

Materials needed

None

Preparing students for success

■ Model gentle hand squeezing before beginning. Practice holding hands without squeezing at all.

■ Practice changing the direction by adding a sound.

How to do it

1. Students sit or stand in a circle and hold hands.

2. Choose a student to be first. Tell the students in which direction to pass the squeeze.

3. The first student passes a gentle hand squeeze to the right (or left) and each student passes it on.

4. When the squeeze has passed all the way around the circle, the first student adds the sound "Ooh" to the squeeze. Each student then says "Ooh" and passes the squeeze until it goes all the way around again.

5. On the next trip around, each student has the option of changing from "Ooh" to "Ahh" or vice versa as they pass the squeeze. Each time the sound changes, the direction of the squeeze (accompanied by the new sound) reverses.

Example:

A silent squeeze is passed to the left all the way around the circle.

The first student adds "Ooh" to the squeeze when it returns to her.

The squeeze and "Ooh" are passed to the left all the way around the circle.

The first student and eight more say "Ooh" as the squeeze continues to the left.

The ninth student says "Ahh" and passes the squeeze to the right.

Thirteen children continue saying "Ahh" and passing the squeeze to the right.

The fourteenth says "Ooh" and passes the squeeze back to the left with students saying "Ooh" until someone changes it again.

Variation

For younger children, you might want to limit the activity to one sound and direction.

Partners and Pairs

An activity that involves silent communication and gentle, safe touching. Students divide into pairs with one sitting and one standing behind. A third person tries to get one of the partners to move. To keep this safe and fun, students need to be familiar with classroom expectations for safe movements, respectful and safe touching, and general good sportsmanship.

Skills practiced

Cooperating; touching safely and respectfully; focus

Materials needed

None

Preparing students for success

- Review class guidelines for safe movements and safe, respectful touching. Model safe movement and gentle touching as needed.
- Remind students that there are no winners or losers.
- Brainstorm and practice some of the silent signals students might use (wink, nod, pointing with a finger, blinking rapidly, etc.).
- Discuss potential problems, for instance, what does it look like to be fully standing?

How to do it

1. Divide the students into two groups—those who will be sitting and those who will be standing. The standing group will have one more person than the sitting group. Since the activity requires an odd number of players, an adult should join in if necessary.

2. Players in the standing group each stand behind a chair in a circle (remove any extra chairs). Players in the sitting group sit in the chairs. There will be one empty chair with a player standing behind it.

3. The player behind the empty chair tries to "recruit" someone to come sit in the empty chair by looking around the circle and using a visual signal (such as a wink, nod, pointing with a finger, etc.) to make contact with a seated player.

4. If a seated player sees the signal, he gets up as quickly as possible and moves to the empty seat. But if the student standing behind him sees the signal also and touches his back before he fully stands up, then he must remain seated.

5. The activity continues until you call time. At any point you can ask sitting and standing groups to switch spots to make the activity more lively.

**Partners
and Pairs**

Grades 2–6

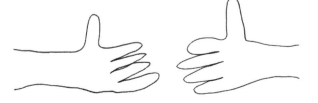

Pass the Chicken

Pass the Chicken

Grades 2–8

A student must name five things that belong in a specified category in the time it takes the others to pass a rubber chicken (or other item) all the way around their circle. The activity is fast-paced and students can play several rounds in five minutes. The activity provides an enjoyable way to review content and develop vocabulary. Everyone wants to beat the chicken!

Skills practiced

Cooperating; gross motor; vocabulary; reviewing content from any area

Materials needed

A yellow rubber chicken purchased at a joke store (or a ball or other soft object)

Preparing students for success

- Brainstorm a list of categories and examples of things in them. For some groups (such as younger children or second-language learners), you may want to post the categories and examples on the board or a chart.

- Practice passing the chicken around the circle in a safe but quick way.

How to do it

1. Students sit in a circle. Choose one student to be "it." That student holds the chicken (or other object).

2. The teacher or a student names a category. The student who is "it" passes the chicken to the right and quickly begins naming things that belong in the category. She must name five things in the category before the chicken makes it all the way around the circle and back to her.

Here are some examples of categories you might use:

- Vocabulary words
- Fruits or vegetables, cereals, desserts, etc.
- Musical instruments, bands or musical groups, songs
- Things you do at school, on weekends, for fun, etc.
- Cartoon characters, story characters, fairy tale characters
- Animals in the jungle, in the sea, on a farm, etc.
- Cities in our state
- States, capitals
- Famous people
- Countries, rivers, mountains
- Sports, sport teams
- Things that . . . grow, are round, are green, float, are made of . . .

3. If the student is able to name five items in the category, another student takes a turn being "it" and repeats the process with a new category. If the student can't name five things, she can have a second chance at being "it" with another category or she can ask another student to be "it."

Password

Students think of synonyms (or brief definitions) for particular words. You can use this activity to build vocabulary, review content from any subject area, or prepare for a test.

Skills practiced

Vocabulary; synonyms; reviewing content

Materials needed

A list of words—new or learned vocabulary words, words related to a unit, words from a word wall, etc.

Preparing students for success

Model and practice how to give synonyms or brief definitions for a word without telling what the word is or using the word itself in the definition.

How to do it

1. One student is "it" and leaves the room or the area.

2. The remaining students in the circle select a word from the list and think of clues they can give to help the student who is "it" to guess the word. Clues should be a single word, such as a synonym, or a short phrase. Brainstorm clues if necessary.

3. The student returns and can call on any student in the circle for a clue. After three to five clues, the student tries to guess the word.

Example:

The group chooses "wise." Students might offer the following clues: "knowledgeable," "intelligent," "knows a lot of things," etc.

4. If the student who is "it" guesses incorrectly, she calls on a student to tell her the word. Regardless of whether she guesses correctly, she chooses another student to be the new "it."

Password

Grades 3–8

Pebble, Pebble

Pebble, Pebble

Grades 1–8

Students say a chant and pass a pebble around the circle. The object is to prevent the person in the middle of the circle from guessing where the pebble is so students work hard to pretend they have the pebble when they don't and vice versa.

Skills practiced

Cooperating; gross motor; oral language; rhythm

Materials needed

One marble, pebble, button, or other small object

Preparing students for success

- Model and practice the action of passing the pebble so no one can tell who has it.
- Practice saying the chant together.

How to do it

1. Students sit on the floor in a circle. Choose one student to move to the middle and be the guesser. The guesser closes her eyes or leaves the area while you give the pebble to one student.

2. The students in the circle begin the chant below while the guesser watches the action closely.

Pebble, pebble,
Where you wander
Up one hill and
Down the other

Is it fair, is it fair
To leave poor _____
(name of guesser)
Just standing there?

3. All students in the circle perform the same action at the same time as they chant—they act as if they are taking a pebble from the hand of the person to their left and moving it to the hand of the person on their right. The goal is to keep the guesser from knowing where the pebble is.

4. After repeating the chant several times, students in the circle stop and hold their arms out straight with closed fists.

5. The guesser is allowed three tries to guess who has the pebble.

Pedoodle

A language game in which students make up sentences that leave out a chosen verb. The game offers good practice for second-language learners and can help everyone review parts of speech and improve vocabulary.

Skills practiced

Vocabulary; sentence structure; parts of speech; deductive reasoning

Materials needed

None

Preparing students for success

- Review appropriate sentences that might be used as clues for a particular word.

- Emphasize the goal of helping each other learn words and practice sentences. The class is trying to help the student guess the correct word, not hide it.

How to do it

1. One student leaves the circle and the class decides on a verb while the student is away, such as "fly."

2. When the student returns, she calls on three different classmates to offer a sentence using the verb chosen by the class. However, classmates will use the word "pedoodle" instead of the chosen verb. For example, if the verb is "read," the sentences might be: "I like to pedoodle long novels." "I'm going to finish pedoodling my book for a book report this weekend." "My parents pedoodle the newspaper every day."

3. After three clues, the student in the middle makes a guess or says she doesn't know and asks for the verb. The student in the middle then chooses another student to be the guesser.

Pedoodle

Grades 2–8

Pros and Cons

Pros and Cons

Grades 4–8

Working with a partner, students take turns quickly listing the positives and negatives (pros and cons) about a topic chosen by the teacher. It is a fast-paced activity that challenges older students to "think on their feet." However, variations can slow the pace so that younger children and second-language learners can do this with greater ease.

Skills practiced

Brainstorming ideas; seeing various sides of an issue; speaking clearly; dealing with time constraints; remembering facts

Materials needed

None

Preparing students for success

■ Select one or more topics for which students will list pros and cons. Students may help you think of topics. Topics can be content-related (being president of the U.S., living in another era, the Civil War, the westward expansion, exploring space, etc.) or concern current events or issues important to students (playing video games, wearing uniforms in school, having a bedtime, etc.). You may also choose more neutral subjects to model the activity or reduce student anxiety (having a pet, what is good/not so good about winter, etc.).

■ Model the activity with more neutral topics before trying controversial topics.

How to do it

1. Assign partners and ask them to scatter around the room. They can either stand or sit. Each pair decides who will be the first caller and who will respond. Announce the first topic for the pro-con activity. When everyone is ready, give a signal to begin.

2. Student A (the caller) claps her hands and says, "Pro!" Student B (the responder) quickly begins naming "pro" or positive things about the topic. After thirty seconds, the teacher signals the students to switch.

3. Student A now claps her hands and says "Con!" Student B now switches to naming "cons" or negatives about the topic. After another thirty seconds, the teacher rings a chime to indicate the end of the first round.

4. Students switch roles but keep the same partner (Student B is the caller and Student A is the responder). You can use the same topic or choose a new one. Ring a chime to begin the second round and a chime to end it, when students return to the circle.

5. Discuss the activity with students and review some of the pros and cons that were shared.

Variations

■ If the activity produces too much anxiety or is too hard for the group, extend the time for responding to a minute or more. You can also have the partners work together to come up with a written list of pros and cons with the teacher serving as the caller for all the partners.

■ Announcing topics ahead of time and brainstorming a few ideas as a group can also make the activity easier.

Pros and Cons

Grades 4–8

"Read All About It" Bingo

"Read All About It" Bingo

Grades K–8

Students circulate and do brief interviews to find students who fit a certain category or know the answers to questions on a bingo sheet. The example here focuses on reading and related activities, but you could also use the activity for content review. The activity must be tailored to fit the age group and requires significant preparation and student self-control.

Skills practiced

Taking turns; asking questions; reading; reviewing content from any area

Materials needed

- Prepare a "bingo sheet" and make copies for every student. Sheets for young students may only be 2 X 2 or 3 X 3, while those for older students may be 5 X 5 or larger. Each square has a written question or category. Younger students may need stickers or pictures to indicate questions and categories. Squares need to be large enough to allow students to sign their initials in them. An example for third graders is shown below.

- A pen, pencil, or marker for each student

Preparing students for success

- Determine and discuss how many answers are needed for "bingo"— all of them, three in a row, etc.

- Review moving safely around the classroom.

- Review how to sign your name with initials, if necessary.

Sample Bingo Sheet:

Reads comic books	Gets books for gifts	Likes to read before bed
Sometimes "reads" the dictionary	Likes books with pictures best	Remembers a favorite book from years ago
Has a favorite author	Reads at least one new book a month	Likes mysteries

How to do it

1. Distribute a "bingo sheet" to each student. When the teacher gives a signal, students mix and mingle to find students who know the answers to the questions or people who fit a category. Students are limited to getting one signature (initials) per person. A student can ask multiple questions, however, in order to get one signature. When a match is found, the student who fits (or answers the question) signs the appropriate box with initials.

2. When a student reaches the specified number and order, the student calls out "Bingo!" You can decide if the activity stops then or continues until more or all students get "Bingo!"

3. After the activity stops, discuss the activity and any interesting information gained.

Variations

■ You can use this activity to review content knowledge, such as math computations, states and capitals, etc.

■ You can use "getting to know you" questions to help build relationships and a sense of community. With older students, this is a good beginning-of-the-year activity.

"Read All About It" Bingo

Grades K–8

The Real Me

A silly guessing game where a student in the middle is blindfolded and tries to guess which classmate made a particular animal noise. A variation allows students to disguise their voices in different ways. Students should be very familiar with everyone's name before playing.

Skills practiced

Active listening; changing pitch of voice

Materials needed

A blindfold

Preparing students for success

- Brainstorm a list of animals and practice the sounds they make.
- Decide and practice what to do if the guesser points to the space between two students.

How to do it

1. Students sit or stand in a circle.

2. Choose one student to be the guesser in the middle. Blindfold the guesser and spin her gently so she doesn't know whom she's facing.

3. The guesser points at the student in front of her and calls out an animal. The student pointed at makes the sound of the animal the guesser called out.

4. The guesser tries to identify which student made the noise. If she guesses correctly, she chooses the next person in the middle. If she is incorrect, the student who made the noise moves to the middle as the next guesser.

Variation

Decide with the children on a simple sentence. Brainstorm a list of ways children can disguise their voices while they say the sentence. For example, students might say the sentence like an excited person, an old person, a much younger child, etc. The guesser spins around, points, and the child he is pointing at says the chosen sentence in a disguised voice. The guesser tries to identify who was speaking.

The Real Me

Grades K–5

Shoes

In this chant, each student has a chance to fill in the blank with a descriptive word. It provides good practice in using descriptive language.

Skills practiced

Vocabulary; rhyming; oral language

Materials needed

None

Preparing students for success

- Model and practice how to tap feet gently on the floor.

- Brainstorm some words to describe shoes (color, kind, condition, material they are made from, etc.) so students have ideas about what they might say when it is their turn.

- Practice the chant before going around the circle.

How to do it

1. Students sit in chairs in a circle so they can gently tap their feet on the floor.

2. Repeat the chant all the way around the circle. When the chant stops for each student, that child gets to use one word to describe his or her shoes. Continue until all students have had a chance to describe their shoes.

Old shoes

New shoes

_____ has

_____shoes!

1, 2, 3, 4!

Gently tap them

On the floor!

Example:

   Old shoes

   New shoes

   Jose has

   (Jose says) Blue shoes!

   1, 2, 3, 4!

   Gently tap them

   On the floor!

Shoes

Grades K–2

Silent Line-Up

Students communicate silently in order to line up in a correct sequence. This silent activity can be used to review academic content and combines the challenges of speed and pantomime.

Skills practiced

Sequencing; nonverbal communication; reviewing any academic content in which sequences are important (such as numbers, steps in a process, historical events)

Materials needed

One index card for each student with information that belongs in a sequence (Roman numerals, alphabetic order for vocabulary, timelines, steps in a process, math facts, fractions, events in a story or history, etc.)

Preparing students for success

Brainstorm some ways to communicate without speaking.

How to do it

1. Distribute cards randomly. Tell students that their challenge is to line up in a particular order using the information on their cards. They must do this silently but they can show each other their cards and they can communicate nonverbally (sign language, gestures, taps on the floor, etc.).

2. Tell students which way to line up (smallest to largest, earliest event to latest, etc.) and challenge them to line up as quickly as possible.

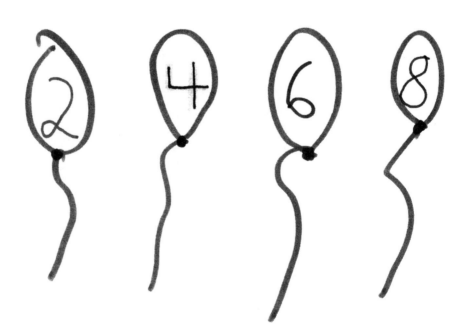

The Sound of Things

A fast-paced guessing game in which students try to guess a word after hearing only a beginning sound and a category. The activity provides practice in phonics and in using categories.

Skills practiced

Identifying beginning sounds of words; categorizing

Materials needed

None

Preparing students for success

- Do a practice run of the activity so students understand what they're supposed to say when they are the leader and what they are trying to guess.

- Brainstorm a possible list of words from a word wall, spelling list, or content area. Post the list where students can easily see it.

How to do it

1. Select a student as leader. The leader chooses a word and says, "I'm thinking of a word that is a thing and it begins with the same sound as 'father'." Possible categories are person, place, or thing.

2. Students raise their hands and the leader calls on them to guess a word that is a thing and begins with that sound. The leader allows three guesses from students and then tells the word if it hasn't been guessed.

3. The activity continues around the circle, with anyone who wants to taking a turn as the leader.

Variation

For younger children, naming a category may not be necessary if word choices are limited.

The Sound of Things

Grades K–4

Syllable Choir

Syllable Choir

Grades 2–5

In small groups, students use single syllables from three-syllable words to sing familiar tunes. When all groups sing the song together, you get a syllable choir!

Skills practiced

Syllabication; active listening; following directions; cooperating

Materials needed

None

Preparing students for success

■ Brainstorm songs to which all students know the melody. Examples are "Row, Row, Row Your Boat" and "Farmer in the Dell."

■ Brainstorm a list of three-syllable words (friendliness, happiness, chocolate, exercise, etc.). With older students, you can use longer words.

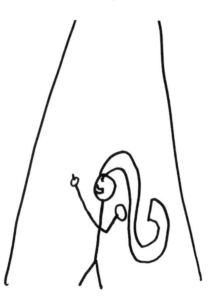

■ Practice singing a song using just one syllable of one of the words (For example, use the first syllable of "happiness" to sing the tune of "Row, Row, Row Your Boat": "Hap, hap, hap hap hap.")

How to do it

1. Select a song and a word as a group.

2. Practice the song (humming is fine) until everyone is comfortable with the tune.

3. Divide students into three groups. Each group will use one syllable of the chosen word to sing the chosen song. For example, if the song is "Row, Row, Row …" and the word is "happiness," one group will sing "hap," another group will sing "i," and the third group will sing "ness."

4. When all three groups are comfortable singing the song with their syllable, everyone sings the song at the same time, each group with their own syllable.

Variation

For older students, one student can leave the room while the group decides on a word and song. When the student returns, he listens to the song and tries to figure out the chosen word. Since all three groups are singing their syllable at the same time, the challenge is to decipher the syllables and put them together into a word.

The Thing in the Bag

Children use pantomime to create an imaginary object from an imaginary ball of clay. Children can be very creative in their choices, but the group needs to be comfortable with pantomime and able to support everyone's efforts for the activity to be successful.

Skills practiced

Making positive comments; nonverbal communication; creative expression; following directions

Materials needed

Paper bag

Preparing students for success

■ Brainstorm a list of possible objects that students could make out of an imaginary ball of clay. The clay can expand and contract as needed to make large and small objects.

■ Model and practice how to make supportive comments.

How to do it

1. Students sit or stand in a circle. Choose a student to begin and place a paper bag in front of that student.

2. The first student pantomimes taking a ball of clay out of the bag and pulling and stretching it to form an object of his choice (a book, for example). He takes some action with the object to indicate what it is (reading the book), then rolls it back into a ball and hands it to his neighbor.

3. The second student follows the same process, using pantomime to create a new object (a baseball) and taking some action to indicate what it is (throwing the ball). She forms a small ball again and hands it to her neighbor.

4. The activity continues until everyone has had a chance. The last person can pantomime rolling the ball up again and putting it in the bag.

5. Discuss the activity, giving each child a chance to name the object s/he created and allowing supportive comments about students' efforts ("Deanna, it looks like you threw that ball with a lot of power.").

The Thing in the Bag

Grades 1–5

Three Clues

Three Clues

Grades 2–8

An activity designed to review familiar content. Students get three clues to help them guess a fact or word.

Skills practiced

Reviewing content; reading; vocabulary

Materials needed

- Index cards with a word or fact related to a familiar content area written on each (countries of the world, vocabulary words, parts of the body, planets, etc.)

- Tape to be used to tape the cards to students' backs

Preparing students for success

- Review the list of words or facts that are written on the index cards. You may want to post the list on the board for reference.

- Model and practice how to give a good clue for a word or a fact.

How to do it

1. Students sit in a circle. Select one student to be "it." This student leaves the circle for a few minutes, moving out of hearing distance.

2. Have a student select a card from the pile and announce the written word or fact (for example, "Amerigo Vespucci").

3. The student who is "it" returns and someone tapes the card to the student's back.

4. The student with the taped card stands in the middle of the circle and asks individual students for a clue (for example, "This person was an explorer."). For some groups, you may want to brainstorm clues before the person who is "it" returns to the circle.

5. The person in the middle can get up to three clues before guessing. If she guesses incorrectly, she can get up to three more clues before removing the card and looking at the correct answer.

6. Select another student to be "it" and follow the same process.

Variation

Working in pairs, students draw a card from a "mystery box." The partners give three clues to the group, who tries to guess the word or fact.

Toe to Toe

An active game for young students that helps teach safe movement and safe touching. When a leader calls out an action, students find a partner and follow the leader's directions for how to stand with their partner. Directions and partners change quickly.

Skills practiced

Following directions; touching respectfully; reviewing names of body parts

Materials needed

None

Preparing students for success

- Brainstorm a list of body parts that leaders can call out.

- Model and practice safe movement around the room.

- Model and practice safe and respectful touching using directions the leader may call out.

- Review the rules of partnering and discuss what happens if there is an odd number (three people can become partners).

How to do it

1. Students stand in a circle. Choose one student to move to the middle and be the leader or "caller."

2. When the leader calls out a direction, students find a partner and follow the leader's directions for how to stand. Possible directions include "toe to toe," "back to back," "elbow to elbow," "heel to heel," etc. Encourage the caller to be creative and use a wide variety of body parts.

3. After everyone is standing with a partner in the correct position, the leader calls out a new direction and students find a new partner.

4. Pace can be rapid but students need to be able to stay safe as they switch partners and stand in new positions.

Variation

For older children, ensure that there is an odd number who are trying to find partners by joining the activity yourself if necessary. When the leader calls out a direction, the student who doesn't find a partner is the new leader.

Toe to Toe

Grades K–2

The Train

A movement activity that combines finding an empty seat (like Musical Chairs) with the repetition of academic information. A fun activity after children are comfortable with each other and with classroom expectations for safe movements.

Skills practiced

Reviewing content information; following directions

Materials needed

A chart to write academic information on

Preparing students for success

- Brainstorm with students a list of names, facts, or vocabulary related to a chosen topic area (states and capitals, body parts, math facts, months, planets, insects, etc.). Post this list. If time is limited, you could prepare the list ahead of time.

- Model safe movements and what to do when two students try for the same seat.

The Train

Grades 3–5

How to do it

1. Students sit in a circle. Assign one item from the list to each student, either verbally or by giving each a card. More than one student can have the same item.

2. Choose one person to be the "caboose" and stand in the middle. Remove that student's chair from the circle.

3. The caboose begins walking around the circle, calling out items from the posted list. The student(s) who has the item called out by the caboose enters the circle and walks in front of the caboose.

4. The process continues until there are four, five, or more students in the "train." The caboose then stops and calls out "Caboose!" and everyone hurries to find a seat. The student without a seat becomes the next caboose and begins the process again.

UFO Experts

Students need to think on their feet as they talk to the class about a common object as if no one had ever seen it before. A great activity to increase verbal skills and encourage creativity and imagination.

Skills practiced

Oral language; vocabulary; creative expression

Materials needed

- A bag or box that can be used to hide an object

- A variety of objects to use as possible "UFOs"—a marker, bottle cap, pebble, CD, brick, can opener, etc.

Preparing students for success

Model the activity before starting so children get a feel for it.

How to do it

1. Choose three students to be the UFO experts. They stand where everyone can see and hear them. Give them the box or bag with the UFO (a common object) in it.

2. They remove the object and consider it. Pretending that this object is something strange that no one has ever seen, their job is to talk about it for two minutes as a group as if they are the experts on explaining UFOs (you can pretend that the class is a TV audience).

3. One student begins talking until she runs out of ideas, then passes the object to the next student, who immediately begins talking about the object and covering new ground. When he is finished, he passes it to student number three, who adds more ideas. If there is time left, the object goes back to the first expert and so on.

4. Begin another round with a new UFO and a new set of experts.

Variation

To make this activity more challenging, or for older students, an area of expertise may be assigned to each member of the team. Roles might include the following:

The Historian—describes the background of the UFO

The Engineer—describes how it is made or used

The Psychologist—describes how it affects people who touch it or use it

The Newscaster—decides what important facts to tell the world about the object

The Grumpy Consumer—a disgruntled user of the UFO who feels it did not perform as it was supposed to

UFO Experts

Grades 3–5

Wadlee Atcha

A silly chant that combines words with a complex set of movements. Students often spontaneously chant this on the playground or at indoor recess.

Skills practiced

Oral language; gross motor; following directions

Wadlee Atcha

Grades K–8

Materials needed

A chart with the words written on it

Preparing students for success

Lead the group through the actions and words. It will take a while before students can lead themselves. You may want to teach it in stages.

How to do it

1. Students stand where they can see you or a student leader. The leader demonstrates the actions while chanting or singing the words.

2. The words go slowly at first and then pick up speed. Modify actions as necessary for different age groups.

Words	Actions
Wadlee atcha	Clap knees (2x), clap hands (2x)
Wadlee atcha	Snap right hand, snap left hand
Doodley do	Grab nose with right hand, then grab right ear with left hand
Doodley do	Grab nose with left hand, then grab left ear with right hand
Wadlee atcha	Clap knees (2x), clap hands (2x)
Wadlee atcha	Snap right hand, snap left hand
Doodley do	Grab nose with right hand, then grab right ear with left hand
Doodley do	Grab nose with left hand, then grab left ear with right hand
It's a simple little song	Clap knees (2x), clap hands (2x)
There's not much to it	Snap right, snap left
All you gotta do is doodley-do it	Clap knees (2x), clap hands (2x), snap right, snap left, grab nose, grab nose
I like the rest but	Clap knees (2x), clap hands (2x)
The part I like best is	Snap right, snap left
Doodley, doodley, doo!	Grab nose, grab nose, clap hands (1x)

Wadlee Atcha

Grades K–8

Watch It

A ball toss activity where students need to pay close attention to each other. It's a good activity to use after they have practiced tossing balls in other activities. Students can invent variations once they have mastered the basics.

Watch It

Grades 6–8

Skills practiced

Gross motor; cooperating

Materials needed

Two small, soft balls like Koosh™ balls

Preparing students for success

Model the activity before playing. Stress the goal of passing the balls without hitting anyone and have students demonstrate gentle tossing so that no one is hurt and others can easily catch the ball.

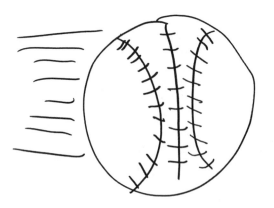

How to do it

1. Students stand in a circle and count off by 2s. The 1s will be throwing a ball to the 1s while the 2s throw another ball to the 2s.

2. Students always toss the ball to the student who is one away from them, skipping the student immediately beside them. As they toss the ball, they say "Watch it!" and make eye contact with the student they are throwing the ball to. The student in between the two who are tossing and catching the ball needs to duck out of the way.

3. The 1s start tossing the first ball. Then the 2s start a second ball in the same direction as the 1s. The goal is to have both balls come back to the first student who threw it.

4. After the first round, discuss successful strategies for getting out of the way and any issues of safety.

Variations

■ Once students master safely passing the ball all the way around the circle with two balls, you can add more balls (an even number).

■ Students can pass two (or more) balls in opposite directions.

■ Students might enjoy inventing variations.

When I Grow Up

A pantomime activity for young students, similar to "It's My Job." It's a good introduction to pantomime and adds to students' knowledge of jobs.

Skills practiced

Nonverbal communication; creative expression; following directions

Materials needed

None

Preparing students for success

- Brainstorm a list of jobs (occupations) and practice pantomiming actions that illustrate something a person in a particular job would do.
- Model the activity before beginning.

How to do it

1. Students sit or stand in a circle. Choose a student to go first. The first student says, "When I grow up I want to be . . . a chef" (or other occupation).

2. The next student in the circle does a brief pantomime of something that a chef would do (such as stirring a pot). It is then her turn to choose a job. She might say, "When I grow up I want to be . . . a ballerina."

3. The next student briefly pantomimes a ballerina's dance and then selects a job and says, "When I grow up, I want to be . . . ."

4. The activity continues around the circle until everyone has had a turn.

Variation

The activity can also be done using actions instead of jobs. For example, a student might say, "When I grow up, I want to . . . read books" or play guitar, drive a race car, build a house, etc.

When I Grow Up

Grades K–2

When Pigs Fly

When Pigs Fly

Grades K–3

A game similar to "Simon Says" where a leader selects one student whose job is to decide if the content of the leader's words is accurate. Other students follow the leader. It's a great game after a trip to the farm or the zoo because it uses animal sounds and motions. Older students can do a more challenging variation that is more like "Simon Says."

Skills practiced

Cooperating; active listening

Materials needed

None

Preparing students for success

- Brainstorm a list of animals and motions or sounds to illustrate what the animals do, such as ducks fly (flapping wings), cats meow (meow sound), dogs bark (barking sound), pigs oink (oinking sound), chickens roost (standing with feet together and knees bent), cows moo (mooing sound), horses trot (running motion), etc.

- Model and practice animal motions and sounds before beginning.

- Also model and practice some incorrect motions and sounds ("Pigs fly" with a flapping motion, for example).

How to do it

1. Students stand in a circle. Choose one student to be the leader.

2. The leader stands in the center and then walks around the circle, stopping before a student. The leader calls out an animal and what it "does" and makes a motion or sound to match. The leader can either match an animal and action correctly ("Horses trot" with a trotting motion) or incorrectly ("Dogs oink" with an oinking sound). All the other students do exactly as the leader does.

3. If the student facing the leader makes a mistake (follows an incorrect action or doesn't follow a correct one), that student becomes the leader. If the student doesn't make a mistake, the leader keeps going around the circle in the same way until someone makes a mistake and becomes the new leader.

4. After the activity is over, review the correct combinations of animals and motions.

Variation

For older students (up to third grade) prepare a number of cards with animal/action combinations written on them, both correct and incorrect. Read the combinations quickly. When someone makes a mistake, that student becomes the new leader and reads the cards.

Where's My Chicken?

A fast-moving activity that involves counting and passing a joke-store rubber chicken around the circle. A low stress activity that helps release tension. Students can play several rounds in five minutes.

Skills practiced

Counting (for lower grades); gross motor; cooperating

Materials needed

A rubber chicken purchased at a joke store

Preparing students for success

Review the rules before beginning, including what happens if someone drops the chicken.

How to do it

1. Students sit in a circle and choose one student to be "it." That student steps out of the circle but stays close and stands with her back to the circle.

2. The student who is "it" begins counting to any number over fifteen and doesn't tell the group to what number she is counting. The students begin passing the chicken very quickly around the circle as soon as the student who is "it" begins counting.

3. When the student who is "it" reaches her chosen number, she shouts, "Chicken!"

4. When students hear "Chicken!" they stop passing it and whoever is holding the chicken is now "it." The first student rejoins the circle.

Where's My Chicken?

Grades K–8

Woof

Woof

Grades K–2

This chant, with accompanying movements, gives young children practice following directions and acting together as a group.

Skills practiced

Cooperating; gross motor; oral language; following directions; rhythm; reading

Materials needed

Large chart with the words of the chant written on it

Preparing students for success

- There needs to be an even number of students. If there is an odd number, you can participate with a student.

- Teach each step slowly before trying to put them all together.

- Write the words on a large chart and post them at the front of the room.

Words	Actions
Bow, wow, wow	Children clap their thighs three times.
Who's got you now?	Children clap each other's hands three times.
Little puppy dog says	Pairs link arms and swing around, changing places.
Bow, wow, wow	Children clap their thighs three times.
WOOF!	Children hop in place turning 180 degrees and facing a new partner.

How to do it

1. Children begin in a circle, standing, facing a partner.

2. With each sentence of the chant, children do the accompanying movement.

3. The chant begins again with a new partner.

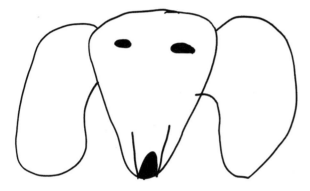

Variations

You could also use the following chants:

Snow, snow, snow
Where is the snow?
Heard the weather show today
Snow, snow, snow
SNOW!

Rain, rain, rain
Where is the rain?
Heard the weather show today
Rain, rain, rain
RAIN!

Sun, sun, sun
Where is the sun?
Heard the weather show today
Sun, sun, sun
SUN!

Woof

Grades K–2

Word Ball

An activity that combines practice with letter sounds with a chant and rolling ball. Students may need some practice rolling the ball safely in the room.

Skills practiced

Gross motor; spelling; letter sounds; oral language; reading

Materials needed

- Large, brightly colored ball
- Word list with words students are learning
- Chart with the words of the chant written on it

Preparing students for success

- Model the activity before beginning, especially rolling the ball safely across the circle.
- Practice the chant until children know it.

Word Ball

Grades K–5

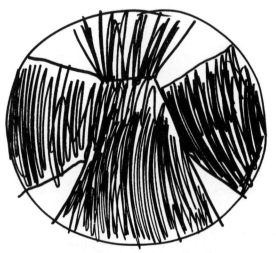

How to do it

1. Students sit in a circle on the floor. Give the ball to the student who will begin the activity.

2. Everyone chants together:

Bouncing through the alphabet with my big [red, blue, green, yellow, orange] ball

Listen so you'll hear the letter that I call

When I say the letter, listen for its sound

And tell a new word as we roll the ball around!

3. When the chant is over, the first student calls out a letter ("C") and rolls the ball across the circle to another student, making eye contact so the receiver knows the ball is coming.

4. The receiver catches the ball and says a word that begins with the chosen letter ("castle").

5. The receiver calls out a new letter and rolls the ball to someone else, and the process is repeated. (Children can say the chant before each student rolls the ball or only once at the beginning.)

Variation

Older children can use blends, endings, rhyming words, etc., instead of beginning letter sounds.

Greetings
to introduce early in the school year

Chicka Boom

A great greeting for learning everyone's name in the first few days or weeks of school. A simple chant with gestures is repeated by the whole class before students use a strong voice to announce their names.

Skills practiced

Learning names; oral language; gross motor; following directions; rhythm

Materials needed

None

Preparing students for success

- Slowly repeat the chant with the gestures a few times until everyone knows it.

- Model and practice using a strong voice to announce names.

How to do it

1. Students sit in a circle. Select one student to be first.

2. Begin the chant below with the whole class.

3. At the end of the chant (after "in our room"), the first student announces her name.

4. The whole class repeats the chant and the next person announces his name.

5. The process is repeated around the circle until all have announced their names.

6. At the end, do the chant a final time, adding the last line, "We are!"

Chicka Boom

Grades K–2

Words	Actions
Chicka chicka	Slap thighs twice.
Boom boom	Clap hands twice.
Look who's here	Slap thighs twice.
In our room	Clap hands twice.
We are! (Last time only)	

Good Day! My Name Is . . .

Students use different languages to greet each other. For older students, try using a new language each day, or tailor your choices to what the class is studying.

Skills practiced

Oral language; appreciating other languages; phonics; accurate pronunciation

Good Day! My Name Is . . .

Grades K–8

"Good day"	Pronunciation
Arabic: Al salaam a'alaykum	Ahl sah-LAHM ah ah-Lay-koom
French: Bonjour	Bohn-ZHOOR
Greek: Kalimera	Kah-lee-MEH-rah
Japanese: Konichiwa	Koh-NEE-chee-wah
Portuguese: Bom dia	Bohn DEE-ah
Swedish: God dag	Goo dahg
"My name is . . ."	**Pronunciation**
Arabic: Ismit	ISS-mee
French: Mon nom or Je m'appelle	Mohn NOHM or ZHUH mah pell
Greek: To honoma moo	Toh HO-no-MA MOO
Japanese: Watakushi-wa (your name), desu	Wah-TAHK-shee-wah (your name), DEHSS
Portuguese: Meu nome	MEH-oo Noh-meh
Swedish: Mitt namn är	Meet nahmn

Materials needed

A list of greetings in other languages, such as the one on the previous page. Many more languages can be found at www.ipl.org/div/kidspace/hello along with recordings of correct pronunciations.

Preparing students for success

- Post the words on the board or a chart and review the pronunciation for the chosen language before beginning. Practice until students feel comfortable with it. For younger students and beginners, start with just saying "Good day" in the foreign language.

- Select a handshake or other gesture to go along with the foreign language greeting.

- Model and practice the phrase and gesture before beginning.

How to do it

1. Students stand or sit in a circle. After reviewing the greeting and gesture, choose a student to go first.

2. The first student turns to the student on his left and uses the phrase and gesture of the day to greet the student: "Good day, _____" or "Good day, my name is …."

3. The student who has been greeted returns the greeting ("Good day, _____" or "Good day, my name is…") and then turns to the person on her left and greets that student. The process continues until all have been greeted.

Variations

- Students may want to find out other words in a particular language to use, such as "peace," "hello," "welcome," etc.

- Students can use other options such as sign language or other kinds of friendly greetings in English, like "Top of the morning," "Howdy," "What's up!" etc.

Good Day! My Name Is …

Grades K–8

Greeting A-Round

Greeting A-Round

Grades K–4

Students repeat a simple chant while moving around in two concentric circles. At the end of each chant, students pause to exchange a friendly greeting with the student in front of them. This greeting provides a chance for students to greet—and be greeted by—many different classmates.

Skills practiced

Oral language; touching safely and respectfully; reading

Materials needed

A chart with the words to the chant written on it

Preparing students for success

- Review what is involved in a friendly greeting (eye contact, using names, gentle handshake, etc.). If necessary, model and practice the basics of a friendly greeting.

- Agree as a class on the one way everyone will greet each other. (Early in the year, a simple "hello" or "good morning" greeting with a handshake is usually best; later students may want to use a more complex greeting.)

- Model and practice how to hold hands and move together in a circle safely.

- Make sure there is an even number of participants.

How to do it

1. Students stand in a circle and count off by 2s.

2. The 2s step forward to form an inner circle.

3. Students in each circle hold hands with their neighbors (1s with 1s, 2s with 2s).

4. Each circle moves in a different direction while students say the following chant:

   Round I go

   Friendly I'll be

   Round and round

   What do I see?

   I see a friend

   Looking at me!

5. When the chant finishes, both circles stop moving and students release their hands. The students in the inner circle (the 2s) turn around to face the students in the outer circle (the 1s).

6. Students in the inner circle greet the student they are facing in the outer circle and vice versa.

7. Students hold hands again (1s with 1s and 2s with 2s), move around in a circle, and repeat the chant. The process continues for five or six rounds.

Knock, Knock

A very simple greeting which uses a "knock, knock" beginning. It's great for learning names and practicing correct pronunciation of first and last names. It works best when students practice safe and respectful touching before beginning.

Skills practiced

Learning names; touching safely and respectfully; oral language; accurate pronunciation

Materials needed

None

Preparing students for success

- Review the simple chant if necessary. Most students will already be familiar with "knock, knock" jokes.

- Model and practice safe and respectful touching. This can involve softly "knocking" a neighbor's shoulder or gently tapping a palm, hand, or shoulder. In some cases, you may prefer students to tap the floor, desk, or chair.

How to do it

1. Students sit or stand in a circle. Choose a student to begin (Amy) who turns to her right, gently "knocks" on her neighbor's shoulder, and uses the chant below to greet him (Sam).

Amy: *Knock, knock!*

Sam: *Who's there?*

Amy: *Amy!*

Sam: *Amy who?*

Amy: *Amy Cruz!*

Class: *Good morning, Amy Cruz!*

2. Sam continues the chant by "knocking" on the student to his right. The greeting continues around the circle until everyone has been greeted.

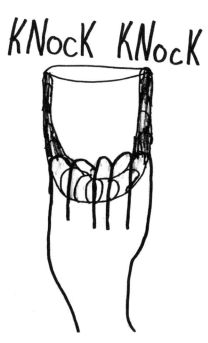

The Name Game

In this timed greeting game, students are challenged to remember everyone's name. Volunteers from the class try to complete the naming in the shortest time possible. The initial focus is to learn names, but a final round can include a more traditional greeting which includes eye contact, a friendly greeting, and possibly a handshake or other gesture.

The Name Game

Grades 3–8

Skills practiced

Learning names; memorizing; working under time pressure; asking for help

Materials needed

A timer of some sort—classroom clock, wristwatch, etc.

Preparing students for success

- Review each student's name before beginning.

- Model and practice a full greeting (eye contact, a friendly voice, etc.) so students are ready to use it in the last round.

- Brainstorm how students might get help if they don't remember a particular name (ask the student, ask the teacher, ask a neighbor, etc.).

How to do it

1. Students stand or sit in a circle. Explain the goal of the game—a number of volunteers will name every student in the circle as quickly as possible. Choose a group of volunteers, perhaps five the first time you do this greeting. Choose a student to start.

2. The first student simply names the student to the left, then continues around the circle, naming each student in turn. When that student is finished, the next volunteer repeats the process.

3. When everyone is done, announce the amount of time it took and challenge the group to improve their time for a second round.

4. The activity ends with students passing a friendly handshake greeting around the circle. The student who went first in the name game begins by turning to the student on his left, shaking her hand, and saying, "Good morning, _____." She then returns the greeting and turns to the person on her left to extend the same greeting.

5. It's important to remind students that the greeting is not timed. The goal now is to greet one another in a friendly way, not to do it as quickly as possible.

Variations

■ Students are seated in a circle. They stand up when their name is called out in the name game, then sit down when their name is called out again.

■ Students try to name a certain number of students in the class without any time pressure. For example, at the end of the first week of school, you might ask, "Who thinks they can name five people in our class?" In the second week, ask for volunteers to name ten people, then fifteen, then twenty, until many students are able to name every person in the class.

The Name Game

Grades 3–8

Photo Greeting

Students choose a card and greet the child whose photo is on the card. It is a particularly good greeting at the beginning of the year for helping children move away from just greeting their friends. It also helps students learn to recognize each other's names in print.

Skills practiced

Name recognition; matching; reading

Materials needed

- A photograph of each child glued to an index card with the name printed beneath the photo.

- A single ring to hold all the cards together.

Preparing students for success

- If necessary, review the basic routines for greeting one another: look the person in the eye, use a friendly voice, and clearly say the person's name and the greeting.

- Show students the photo ring and model how to find the person in the group and greet him in a friendly way. Also, model what to do if you need help reading the name.

How to do it

1. Students either sit or stand in a circle.

2. The person who begins finds her photo in the ring of cards and flips it to the end. She then greets the next person on the ring by walking over to that person and saying, "Good morning, _____." The person returns the greeting, "Good morning, _____."

3. The first greeter hands the ring of cards to the person she greeted and goes back to her spot in the circle.

4. The new greeter flips his name to the end and greets the next person on the ring. This continues until everyone has been greeted.

5. Afterwards, mix up the cards so they'll be in a different order for the next time.

6. If a child is absent, the person whose turn it is can greet that child by saying, "Good morning, _____. We're thinking of you." The child then goes on to greet the next person on the ring.

What's Your Name?

This is a basic greeting. It helps students learn fundamental greeting skills such as making eye contact, greeting in a friendly and strong voice, offering a handshake, etc. Once students are familiar with everyone's name, variations listed here and on other pages can be used to add interest, complexity, and fun.

Skills practiced

Friendly greeting; oral language; listening

Materials needed

None

Preparing students for success

Teach and model expectations for greeting others before beginning. Include making eye contact, greeting in a friendly and strong voice, and offering a handshake or other gesture.

How to do it

1. Students sit or stand in a circle. Select a student to begin.

2. The first student turns to the neighbor on the right (or left) and uses the basic greeting below:

First student: *"Hello (or Hi). My name is _____. What's your name?"*

Second student: *"Hello (or Hi), _____. My name is _____."*

First student: *"Hello (or Hi), _____."*

Students then shake hands or do another greeting gesture.

The second student then turns to the next student in the circle and begins the greeting again: *"Hello (or Hi), _____. What's your name?"*

3. The process is repeated around the circle until everyone is greeted.

Example:

1. The first student (Daniel) turns to the student to his right and says, "Hi. My name is Daniel. What's your name?"

2. The student to the right responds, "Hello, Daniel. My name is Beth."

3. Daniel says, "Hello, Beth." They shake hands.

4. Beth then turns to her right and says to the next child, "Hello, my name is Beth. What's your name?"

5. That child says, "Hello, Beth. My name is Angel." Beth says, "Hello, Angel." Beth and Angel shake hands.

6. The greeting continues around the circle until it returns to Daniel.

Variations

- Students can use other gestures besides handshakes—a wave, high five, etc.

- Other kinds of greetings or questions can be used, such as "Hi, Celia. I'm glad you're here." "Good morning, Elizabeth. How are you?" or "What's your name and what do you do?" (I'm a student, a writer, a reader, a soccer player, your classmate, etc.) Brainstorm possible answers to questions before beginning.

What's Your Name?

Grades K–3

Greetings
to introduce later in the school year

Around the Circle Hello

Students walk, skip or hop around the outside of the circle before choosing a student to greet. That student then uses the same type of movement but travels in the opposite direction until the two meet and greet.

Skills practiced

Gross motor; noticing

Materials needed

None

Preparing students for success

- Review safe movements in the classroom.

- Decide on a type of movement that will be used by students in moving around the outside of the circle. Older students can brainstorm and select their own.

- Decide on a greeting format.

- Establish a sign to show who has been greeted (thumbs up, raised hand, etc.).

How to do it

1. Students stand in a circle with enough room for someone to pass behind them. Choose a student to be the first greeter.

2. The greeter moves out of the circle and walks (or uses any other movement that has been agreed on, such as hopping, skipping, etc.) around the outside of the circle to the right (or left).

3. The greeter chooses a student to greet and taps the student on the shoulder. That student backs up and moves around the circle in the opposite direction, using the same type of movement (walking, hopping, etc.).

4. When the two students meet, they greet each other in the specified way. The first student returns to her place in the circle and makes the designated motion to show she has been greeted (folds her arms, raises her hand, etc.).

5. The second student becomes the next greeter, moving around the circle and choosing a student to greet.

6. The process is repeated until everyone has been greeted.

Around the Circle Hello

Grades K–8

Baseball Greeting

The language of baseball hits—singles, doubles, triples, and home runs—is used to make this greeting lively and interesting. Students need to understand the terms before beginning.

Skills practiced

Counting; touching safely and respectfully

Materials needed

A chart with baseball terminology written on it

Preparing students for success

- Review baseball terminology with students. Explain and post the following definitions:

  Single = one base

  Double = two bases

  Triple = three bases

  Home run = four bases

- Review safe and respectful touching and model and practice high fives, low fives, handshakes, etc., as necessary.

- Establish a signal to identify students who have already been greeted— thumbs up, arms crossed, etc.

- Do a practice round before doing the greeting for the first time.

Baseball Greeting

Grades 2–8

How to do it

1. Students stand in a circle. Choose a student to be first. That student decides and announces what type of hit she's made (single, double, etc.).

2. She then turns to her right and begins to walk around the inside of the circle. Each student she passes represents a base. For example, the child to her right is first base, the next child is second base, etc.

3. She "high fives" or "low fives" the students on the bases she passes before coming to her designated base. For example, if she "hit" a triple, she high fives the two students to her right and then stops at the third child. She greets him in the designated way ("Good morning, ___" with a handshake, for instance) and takes his place in the circle.

4. The child who was greeted then becomes the new hitter. He repeats the process except that now when he takes the place of the student he greets, he makes the designated motion to show that he's already been greeted (fold arms, sit down, etc.).

5. The process continues with subsequent "hitters" skipping those who have already been greeted. That is, students who have been greeted no longer count as bases.

6. The process continues until everyone in the circle has been greeted. The last person to be greeted will be the person who was the first hitter.

Bead Exchange

Students greet students who are holding different beads (or other small objects) than they are. Greetings can be marked by the exchanging of beads. This greeting can also be used to form two groups. All the students holding a certain color bead at the end of the greeting come together to form a group.

Skills practiced

Friendly greeting; gross motor

Materials needed

Enough beads (or other small objects such as counters, chips, etc.) so that each student gets one; (half should be one color and the other half another color)

Preparing students for success

- Review safe movements in the classroom before beginning.

- Review expectations for greetings before beginning—eye contact, a friendly and strong voice, handshake, etc.

How to do it

1. Students stand in a circle. Give each student a bead.

2. Give a signal for students to mix and mingle, greeting students who have a different color bead. When the greeting is complete, the students exchange beads.

3. The process continues with students always looking for someone with a different color bead.

4. After about two minutes, give a signal for the greeting to end.

Bead Exchange

Grades K–8

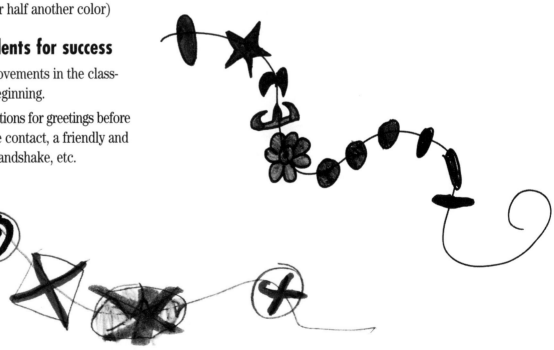

Calling All Friends

Calling All Friends

Grades 2–8

Students select a descriptive adjective or another word to go along with their first names and other students are challenged to remember it. Students are encouraged to use words creatively. Variations can provide a review of academic content.

Skills practiced

Active listening; concentrating; descriptive language; alliteration

Materials needed

None

Preparing students for success

- Establish a familiar sign to show who has been greeted (thumbs up, raised hand, etc.).

- Brainstorm words students can use which fit the guidelines you choose. For example, you might specify adjectives which start with the same letter as students' first names, words describing personal interests, science or math vocabulary, rhyming words, etc.

- Discuss what students can do if they don't remember a student's word or name (ask the student, ask other students, get a hint, etc.).

How to do it

1. Students sit in a circle. Each student thinks of a word which fits the guidelines you have established.

2. When everyone is ready, select a student to go first and announce the word which goes with her name (such as Joyful Jennifer, Gymnast Linda, Amoeba Annie, Jill Brazil, etc.). Each student repeats the process around the circle. The goal is for students to try to remember the words for several classmates, not all of them.

3. Select a student to begin the greeting. He chooses a student and greets her in the following way: "Careful Carlos calling Merry Maria. Good morning, Maria." She responds, "Good morning, Careful Carlos" and then repeats the process ("Merry Maria calling Quick Quincy. Good morning, Quincy.").

4. The process is repeated until everyone has been greeted.

Variations

- Brainstorm different types of words to use, such as verbs, adverbs, favorite things, content vocabulary, words in a different language, etc.

- Second-language learners can write their word on a card and show it to the greeter.

Category Greeting

A quick and fun greeting which allows everyone to be greeted in the time it usually takes for just four greetings. When a category is called out, all students who fit the category enter the circle and greet each other. After three categories, anyone who has not entered the circle yet does so.

Skills practiced

Categorization; friendly greeting

Materials needed

None

Preparing students for success

- Brainstorm with the students three categories for the day. Some examples are students who wear glasses, were born in the spring, who had cereal for breakfast this morning, who have more than five first cousins, whose favorite color is blue, whose favorite food is pizza, etc. You can simply announce the categories for the day if you need to save time.

- As necessary, review expectations for greetings before beginning—eye contact, a friendly and strong voice, a handshake if desired, etc.

- Model and practice the activity as necessary before beginning.

How to do it

1. Students stand in a circle. The teacher or leader calls out a category.

2. All students who fit the category move into the circle and greet each other in the designated way. When every student has greeted every other student in the group, they all move back to their places in the circle.

3. The process is repeated for two other categories, with students only entering the circle one time. (If they fit more than one category, they only enter the circle the first time.)

4. After three categories, the teacher or leader calls out, "Anyone who has not greeted yet!" and any remaining students enter the circle and greet each other.

Category Greeting

Grades K–8

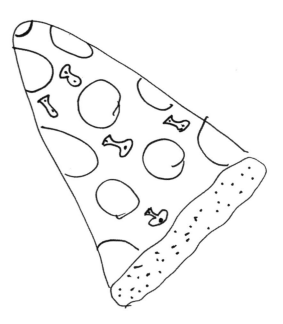

Choice Greeting

Choice Greeting

Grades K–8

After students are skilled in basic types of greetings, this greeting offers them a choice of three types from which to choose. Students are often interested in inventing new options for this greeting as well.

Skills practiced

Choice making; creative expression; safe and respectful touching

Materials needed

None

Preparing students for success

■ Review expectations for greetings before beginning—eye contact, a friendly and strong voice, a hand-shake, etc.

■ Review safe and respectful touching.

■ Establish a signal to show a student has been greeted if greetings move back and forth across the circle or are random.

How to do it

1. Students stand in a circle. Explain that they can choose any of the three (or two for younger students) greeting options specified. Here are three examples:

Hey, _____! with a rainbow wave (hand moves in an arc, the shape of a rainbow)

Yo, _____! with a handshake where the fingers of the right hand are curled and hooked with the curled fingers of the other person

What's up, _____! with a high five

2. Decide on which direction the greeting will travel (right, left, across the circle, random, etc.) and choose a student to begin.

3. The first student makes eye contact with the student to be greeted and uses one of the three greeting options, moving closer if necessary. The greeted student responds with the same greeting and motion.

4. The second student repeats the process, using one of the three options. The process continues until all have been greeted.

Variations

■ Brainstorm with students new and different greeting options, including words and gestures.

■ Students wait to do the gesture which goes along with the words so they both do it at once. For example, "Hey, Yolanda!" "Hey, Ramon!" and then both do the rainbow wave at the same time.

Did You Know . . .?

Students greet one another while passing an object around the circle and providing a brief piece of information about it. This greeting works best in smaller groups so that information about the object isn't exhausted. It can also be used to review academic content.

Skills practiced

Oral language; sentence construction; building general knowledge; reviewing academic content

Materials needed

An object to pass around the circle such as a soft stuffed animal (a student favorite), a plastic farm animal, a card with a picture, a small figure such as a deep sea diver or other person related to a story or content area, etc.

Preparing students for success

- Brainstorm some "things you know" about the prop that will be passed around.

- Model and practice "telling something you know" in a sentence before beginning.

- Explain that it is okay if several students think of the same question to ask.

How to do it

1. Students sit in a circle. Display the prop that will be passed around and give students a minute to think of something they know about it.

2. When everyone is ready, choose a student to begin and hand her the prop. Students greet the student next to them and then add a fact about the prop in the "Did you know . . . ?" format. This example uses a stuffed chicken.

Allie: *Good morning, Brett. Did you know chickens have feathers?*

Brett: *Good morning, Allie. Yes, I know.*

Brett: *Good morning, Kalia. Did you know chickens lay eggs?*

Kalia: *Good morning, Brett. Yes, I know.*

Kalia: *Good morning, Orlando. Did you know a baby chicken is called a chick?*

Orlando: *Good morning, Kalia. Yes, I know.*

3. The process continues until everyone has been greeted.

Variations

- Use a variety of props to pass around. They may be related to academic content such as a dinosaur, a picture from a field trip, a figure from a particular occupation, etc.

- This greeting can be changed to an activity simply by omitting the greeting part of the conversation.

Did You Know...?

Grades K–2

The Farmer Calls

Once students are familiar with the expectations for greetings, this is a fun way to break into small groups and practice friendly greetings. Students make animal noises which match the cards they've been given and find others students making the same sounds. Once they are grouped, students greet each other.

The Farmer Calls

Grades K–2

Skills practiced

Active listening; moving safely around the classroom; following directions

Materials needed

Index cards with names, pictures, or stickers of familiar animals. You'll need one for each student and two to four of each animal.

Preparing students for success

- Review safe movements around the room before beginning.

- Review the animals on the cards and the sounds they make before beginning. Model and practice the sounds as necessary.

- As necessary, review expectations for greetings before beginning—eye contact, a friendly and strong voice, handshake, etc.

How to do it

1. Students stand or sit in a circle. Give each student a card with an animal on it.

2. When all students have a card, they begin to move around the circle making the sound of the animal on the card.

3. Students identify other students making the same sound and form a group— all of the pigs together, all of the cows, ducks, chickens, etc.

4. Students continue making their sounds until all groups are formed. Ring a chime or make a signal for the noises to stop and for students to greet the others in their group. Each child takes a turn saying hello and offering a handshake (or other form of greeting) to every other child in the group.

5. When the greetings are complete, you become the "farmer" and call out each animal in turn to come back to the barn (their seats in the circle). The pigs oink when you call on them until they get back to their seats. This continues until all the animals have been called.

Variation

Vary the sounds used to group children. For example, you might use sounds for letters in the alphabet; sounds for cars, airplanes, trains, etc.; or even familiar tunes (students hum the tunes to find one another).

Galaxy Greeting

A greeting which uses the theme of outer space travel to allow students to mix and greet each other randomly. Students get to act out how they imagine space travelers move and talk. Variations can use different creative themes. Students should already be comfortable with expectations for greetings and know everyone's name.

Skills practiced

Following directions; creative expression; moving safely around room

Materials needed

None

Preparing students for success

- Review safe movements in the classroom.

- Brainstorm ideas for how space travelers might move and talk.

- Decide on a greeting format and model and practice it before beginning as necessary.

- Make sure there is an even number of participants.

How to do it

1. Students sit or stand in a circle. Explain that they will be pretending to be astronauts (or creatures from outer space) traveling through space. They will greet each other, without touching, in the designated way.

2. Give a signal for everyone to begin. Students mix and mingle, walking as if in space and being careful not to bump into another astronaut (or "space being") or the furniture (planets or space ships).

3. Each student makes eye contact with another space traveler. The two students greet one another by saying, "Greetings, _____! May the force be with you" (or "Live long and prosper" or "Peace in the universe," etc.).

4. After one greeting is complete, each student moves on to greet another traveler.

5. After each student has greeted three or four others, give a signal for the greeting to end and for all space travelers to move slowly and carefully back to the circle.

Variation

Brainstorm ideas for other themes to use, such as Halloween (ghost greeters), Egypt (mummy greeters), ocean explorers (scuba diver greeters), etc.

Galaxy Greeting

Grades K–3

Greeting Braid

This greeting requires concentration and may take some practice to get the movements right. In the end, the class is "braided" together by their arms.

Skills practiced

Moving safely; focus; cooperating

Materials needed

None

Preparing students for success

- Review and model respectful touching and safe movements.

- Make sure there is an even number of participants.

How to do it

1. Students stand in a circle and count off by 2s.

2. The 1s step forward to form an inner circle. The 1s turn to face the students in the outer circle and hold hands (1s with 1s).

3. The 2s make an outer circle and hold hands. They should step forward so they are close to the inner circle and move just slightly to the right so that each student is facing a pair of linked hands.

4. Choose a student in the inner circle to begin the greeting. She turns to the student in the outer circle standing just to her right and greets him by saying, "Good morning, Tony." Tony responds, "Good morning, Sonya."

5. The first student (Sonya) and the student she is holding hands with in the inner circle (Matt) lift their linked hands over Tony's head and bring them down behind his back and leave them there.

6. The greeting continues with the next student in the inner circle repeating the process. After all students in the inner circle have greeted the student on their right in the outer circle, the two groups will be "braided" together.

7. If there's time, the group can "unbraid"— students from the outer circle (the 2s) greet students from the inner circle and the students in the inner circle bring their arms back in front of the students in the outer circle.

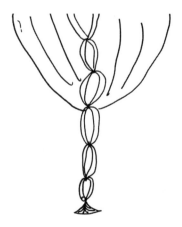

High Five/Ankle Shake

A combination greeting that requires students to cooperate with one another in order to make the movements successful. It also mixes up the seating order in the meeting circle.

Skills practiced

Cooperating; following directions; respectful touching

Materials needed

None

Preparing students for success

- Review respectful touching.
- Model the greeting and ask students for ideas for helping each other stay safe.

How to do it

1. Children stand in a circle and the teacher chooses someone to go first. This person walks over to a person across the circle and stands next to the person. The greeter says, "Good morning, _____" and the person returns the verbal greeting.

2. The two students then do a high five while gently "shaking" each other's ankle at the same time. To do the ankle shake successfully, students bend slightly at the waist and lift the leg closest to their partner, bending at the knee. This allows easy access to the other person's ankle. To help balance, students can gently place one of their hands on the other student's shoulder while doing the high five.

3. After the greeting is completed, the first greeter stays in her new spot in the circle. The person who was greeted now chooses someone else in the circle to greet.

4. Once a student has been greeted, he uses the designated motion (sit down, fold arms, etc.) to show this.

5. The greeting continues until every student has been greeted.

Variations

- To make the greeting simpler, students can just do the ankle shake.

- Younger students enjoy a variation of this, called Footsies Greeting, where students sit down, face one another, and gently place their feet together (sole to sole) while greeting each other by name.

- Hip-Hop/High Five: In this variation, children greet each other with a high-five and a gentle bump to the hip. Modeling of respectful touching is essential for this activity.

High Five/ Ankle Shake

Grades 3–8

Hullabaloo Greeting

Sometimes known as the "confusion greeting," this is an active greeting that requires adequate space and a good deal of self-control. Students move around the classroom in a variety of ways, greet one another in a variety of ways, and share a piece of information about themselves. The combination of the three can create quite a "hullabaloo."

Skills practiced

Moving safely around room; cooperation; following directions; gross motor

Materials needed

A poster or chart with brainstormed ideas for each category (see sample below)

Preparing students for success

- The greeting works best if the teacher or leader says the directions in this order: how to move, how to greet, what topic to share. Do a practice round or two with students as necessary.

- Discuss and model how to move around the room safely.

- Remind students that the purpose of activity is to greet one another in a friendly way, so that this focus is not lost in the fun of the activity.

- Make sure there is an even number of participants.

Sample Chart

Ways to move	Ways to Greet	Topics to share
Tip toe	Link elbows	Favorite dessert
Skip	Handshake	Number of kids in family
Walk like a mummy	Pinky shake	A favorite book
"Swim"	High five	A favorite activity
Etc.		

How to do it

1. Students stand in a circle. A leader calls out three directions in quick succession, one from each category. For example, the leader might call "Hop, high five, favorite ice cream flavor."

2. Students move about the room in the designated way (hop), find a partner, and greet that person in the designated way (high five).

3. After greeting each other, partners share one piece of information about themselves, using the category that has been named (favorite ice cream flavor).

4. The leader rings a bell to signal the beginning of the next round and calls out three new directions. Students move in the designated way to find a new partner.

5. This continues for three or four rounds. When the leader rings the bell after the last round she tells students to go back to their meeting spots.

6. After doing this greeting the first few times, briefly reflect with students about what made it fun, successful, or safe. Ask students to share ideas for improvement.

Hullabaloo Greeting

Grades 3–8

Jump In, Jump Out

A chant for younger students which involves physical action and a group greeting. It's a good energizer in the morning for groups smaller than twenty.

Skills practiced

Gross motor; following directions; reading

Materials needed

A chart with the words to the chant written on it

Preparing students for success

- Review safe movements in the classroom before beginning. Model and practice jumping in, jumping out, and spinning safely.

- Review the words to the chant as needed.

How to do it

1. Students stand in a circle. Select a student to go first.

2. The group repeats the chant below while the first student performs the actions.

3. The process is repeated around the circle until everyone is greeted.

Jump In, Jump Out

Grades K–2

Words	Actions
Group: *Jump in*	First student jumps toward middle of the circle.
Group: *Jump out*	Student jumps backward to previous spot in circle.
Group: *Turn yourself about*	Student spins around until facing in again.
Group: *We want to know your name So please call it out*	
Student responds: *Michael!*	
Group responds: *Good morning, Michael!*	

Moving Name

Students use a simple motion to accompany each syllable of their name. It's a great way to understand and review syllables and allows each student to choose a motion which the class will repeat.

Skills practiced

Syllabication; gross motor; memory

Materials needed

None

Preparing students for success

- Brainstorm simple motions which can be used. Examples include clapping high or low, snapping fingers, patting thighs, tapping the belly or top of the head, etc.

- Review syllables as needed. Practice with a few names before beginning.

How to do it

1. Students stand in a circle. Review how many syllables are in each student's name by quickly going around the circle and saying and clapping the syllables in each name.

2. Have students decide on a motion to go with their syllables.

3. When all students indicate they are ready, choose a student to go first.

4. The first student calls out the syllables of her name, repeating the motion she has chosen with each syllable (for example, "Tam-a-ra," snapping her fingers three times).

5. The class greets her, "Good morning, Tam-a-ra," using the same motion when saying her name.

6. The process is repeated until all have called out their names.

Variation

When students have mastered the greeting, challenge them to remember as many motions as possible by going back around the circle from last to first, repeating the names and motions as a group.

Moving Name

Grades K–3

Shoe Twister Greeting

Students take off a shoe and make a pile in the center. Each student chooses a shoe from the pile and returns it to its owner, greeting that person in the process. The greeting is fun and silly, as everyone stands with only one shoe on and each greeter must search for a matching shoe by staring at everyone's feet.

Skills practiced

Matching; friendly greeting

Materials needed

None

Preparing students for success

- Decide on a greeting format before beginning. Model and practice it as necessary.

- Model and practice the game before beginning with special emphasis on gently handing the shoe to the owner.

How to do it

1. Students stand in a circle, take off one shoe, and place their shoe in the center of the circle. Students return to their place in the circle.

2. Call out "Shoe twister" and all students move to the center of the circle, take a shoe from the pile (not their own), and return to their previous place.

3. Choose a student to be the first greeter. That student looks at the shoe she's holding and searches the circle until she finds the owner of the matching shoe. She returns her shoe to that student and they greet each other in the chosen format.

4. The next student repeats the same process and greetings continue until all have been greeted.

Silent Signal Greeting

After students know everyone's name, they choose gestures to represent their names in this completely silent greeting. It's a challenge for them to remember everyone's gesture and satisfying when they do. The silence is a nice change of pace and may help some students concentrate.

Skills practiced

Concentration; gross motor; memory

Materials needed

None

Preparing students for success

■ Brainstorm different kinds of gestures students might use to represent their names (tugging on their right ear, scratching their head, a salute, raising their arms over their head, etc.). Each student needs a unique gesture. Discuss what to do if one student uses a gesture another had planned to use.

■ Discuss, model, and practice ways to silently ask for help if a student cannot remember another student's gesture.

■ Establish a sign to show who has been greeted (thumbs up, raised hand, etc.).

■ Model and practice the greeting before beginning.

How to do it

1. Students sit or stand in a circle. Remind them that the game is silent and give them a moment to choose a gesture to represent their names.

2. When everyone is prepared, choose a student to go first and then go around the circle twice with students demonstrating the gesture they've chosen. Everyone's goal is to remember as many as possible.

3. Choose a student to begin the greeting by making eye contact with someone across the circle. The first student waves and then does that student's gesture. The student being greeted waves back and does the greeter's gesture. Students can get help from other students if they are having trouble remembering a student's gesture.

4. The second student repeats the process by greeting someone else across the circle. The process continues until everyone has been greeted.

5. Take a few minutes to reflect on this activity afterwards, noting successes and challenges.

Variations

■ Ask each student to do a gesture that represents an interest, hobby, or sport (playing basketball, reading, gardening, etc.). Students can share their interests verbally at the end of the greeting.

■ If students have learned how to say "Hello!" or "Good morning" in American Sign Language, they can use these signs instead of waving.

Silent Signal Greeting

Grades 3–8

Snake Greeting

After students are familiar with a variety of greeting gestures, this activity gives them the opportunity to choose their own unique way of greeting others. In the process, a "snake" forms in the center of the circle.

Skills practiced

Creative expression; touching safely and respectfully; active listening

Materials needed

None

Snake Greeting

Grades 3–8

Preparing students for success

- Students should be familiar with a variety of greetings. Review greetings that have been learned and brainstorm possible combinations of words and gestures before beginning.

- Because there are many students greeting at once in this activity, it's important to review ways to keep the noise at an acceptable level before beginning. To keep the noise level down, you may want to limit greetings to silent signals or have students whisper their greetings.

How to do it

1. Students stand in a circle and think of how they would like to greet others. When each student is prepared with their own way of greeting others, select a student to begin.

2. The first student moves to the student on his left and greets her with his unique greeting. She then greets him using the same words and gesture.

3. The first student then continues around the circle, repeating the process. The second student follows the first and uses her own unique greeting. The third student follows the second, etc. This continues right around the circle, forming a "snake" in the middle.

4. When the first student returns to his place in the circle, he takes his place again and the snake then greets him as it passes. Students return to their places in the circle in turn. When all students have returned to their places, each will have greeted and been greeted by everyone.

Example:

1. Jack is first and greets Sheri on his left with "Jambo, Sheri!" and a handshake. Sheri repeats, "Jambo, Jack" and returns the handshake.

2. Jack moves on to Victor and repeats his "Jambo!" greeting and Victor repeats it back.

3. Sheri follows Jack and greets Victor, "Top of the morning, Victor!" and gives him a salute. Victor repeats, "Top of the morning, Sheri!" and returns her salute.

4. Sheri moves on to greet the next person in line. Then Victor follows Sheri and also greets the next student in line with his own unique greeting.

5. When Jack gets back to his place in the circle, he takes his place again. Sheri then greets him with "Top of the morning, Jack" and her salute. He repeats her greeting.

6. Sheri returns to her place in the circle. Victor greets Jack and Sheri in turn, and then returns to his place in the circle. This continues until everyone is back in his/her original place.

Snake Greeting

Grades 3–8

The Squeeze

The Squeeze

Grades 3–8

Students mingle in the center of the circle and offer handshake greetings to as many classmates as possible. Meanwhile, two students, secretly chosen by the teacher, offer an extra squeeze with their handshakes. Classmates are challenged to figure out the identity of the secret squeezers. After students master the basic activity, variations can add an extra challenge.

Skills practiced

Observation; friendly greeting

Materials needed

None

Preparing students for success

- Review expectations for greetings—eye contact, a friendly and strong voice, handshake, etc.

- Model and practice a gentle "double squeeze" in a handshake which will be used as the secret signal.

- Brainstorm ideas for how to identify the squeezers (for example, watch others closely to see which students have shaken a kneeling student's hand).

How to do it

1. Students stand or sit in a circle and close their eyes. The teacher walks around the circle and secretly taps two students who will become the "squeezers."

2. Students open their eyes. All students then mix and mingle, greeting others with a handshake and a friendly hello at random.

3. The "squeezers" randomly use a gentle double squeeze in their handshake with some of the students as they greet them. When a student's hand has been double squeezed, that student kneels on the floor. After four or five students are kneeling, stop the activity and ask if anyone wants to guess the identity of the squeezers.

4. The students who are still standing raise their hands to make a guess. If a student guesses incorrectly, that student also kneels.

5. After the "squeezers" are discovered, new "squeezers" can be chosen for another round.

Variations

- To increase the challenge, students who have been "squeezed" can silently count to three before kneeling down.

- Students can use other signals to show they have been "squeezed"—holding up a hand, crossing their arms, calling out "Squeezed!" etc.

- Students can use a wink, a nod, etc., instead of a squeeze.

2-4-6-8

A simple chant and activity which allows the whole group to greet each student. It is also a way to energize the group and let off a little steam. The chant works best in groups smaller than twenty.

Skills practiced

Oral language; rhythm; safe and respectful touching

Materials needed

None

Preparing students for success

- Review expectations for safe and respectful touching. Model and practice an appropriate "high five."

- Model how loud the clapping and chant should be so other classes aren't disturbed. Practice the chant before beginning.

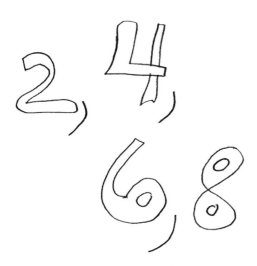

How to do it

1. Students stand in a circle. Students repeat the chant below, clapping four beats for each line. The chant is repeated until each student has been named.

2, 4, 6, 8!

Who do we appreciate?

Sam, Sam

Yeah, Sam!

2. As the last line of the chant ("Yeah, Sam!") is said, the named student proceeds around the interior of the circle giving every student a "high five," similar to the way players greet each other at the end of a baseball game, until he gets back to his place in the circle.

3. Each student can try to finish high-fiving everyone in the circle before the chant is completed. However, if this isn't possible, it's fine to just begin the chant again and name the next student. The second student will then begin giving high-fives in the circle while Sam is finishing up.

4. The chant continues until everyone has been named.

Variation

Students can try other gestures to greet students around the circle—a "low five," bumping fists gently, double "high five," etc.

The Weekend Is Near

A chant is combined with pantomime movements in this greeting. Each student is named by the group and acts out a favorite weekend activity. The greeting can be made more challenging for older students by asking them to repeat previous students' choices.

Skills practiced

Creative expression; oral language; memory; reading

Materials needed

A chart with the words to the chant written on it

Preparing students for success

- Brainstorm a variety of weekend activities and pantomime movements to match them. Model and practice this as necessary.
- Practice the chant before beginning.

The Weekend Is Near

Grades K–8

Words	Actions
Group: *Hello, Sara!* *The weekend is near*	Everyone waves at Sara.
What are you gonna do	Everyone points at Sara.
When it really gets here?	Everyone points down to the floor on the word "here."
Sara says: *I'm gonna read, read, read*	She pretends to read a book.
Group responds: *She's gonna read, read, read*	Everyone pretends to read a book.

How to do it

1. Students stand or sit in a circle. Select a person to be named first.

2. Everyone says the chant together. The student who is named answers the question with an action verb (such as read, swim, play, sleep, etc.) and a pantomime action, which the group then repeats.

3. The chant continues around the circle until everyone has been named.

4. At the end, try going around the circle and repeating as a group what each person said and pantomimed. For example, Sara's going to read, read, read; Tim is going to sleep, sleep, sleep; etc.

Variation

Older students can be challenged to repeat the activities and actions of the last five students after they have taken their own turn—Walter's going to dance, dance, dance; Greta's going to phone, phone, phone; etc.

The Weekend Is Near

Grades K–8

Welcome Chant

A chant for younger students which involves clapping and greeting each student as a group. The words reinforce a welcoming attitude.

Skills practiced

Oral language; rhythm; reading

Materials needed

A chart with the words to the chant written on it

Welcome Chant

Grades K–2

Preparing students for success

- Review the words to the chant as needed.
- Model and practice using a warm and welcoming voice in the chant.

How to do it

1. Students stand in a circle. Select one student to be greeted first (Marika).

2. The group uses the following chant, clapping as they say the words.

Here's to Marika! (Marika takes a step forward into the circle.)

She's welcome in our room!

Here's to Marika!

She's welcome in our group!

Good morning, Marika!

Marika responds: *Good morning, friends!*

Marika steps back into her place in the circle.

3. The process continues around the circle until everyone has been greeted.

What's the News?

Here, a greeting is combined with the sharing portion of Morning Meeting. It can be used to share "personal" news or as a way to review academic content or current events.

Skills practiced

Public speaking; active listening; reviewing academic content or current events

Materials needed

None

Preparing students for success

- As needed, review expectations for greetings before beginning—eye contact, a friendly and strong voice, a handshake if desired, etc.

- As needed, review expectations and guidelines for sharing—a limit of one or two sentences, appropriate topics, how to pass ("No news today"), etc.

- Select a type of sharing for the day (such as personal news, facts about something the class is studying, current events, etc.).

How to do it

1. Students sit in a circle. After reviewing guidelines for greeting and sharing, select a student to go first.

2. The first student turns to his left, greets that student, and asks, "What's the news?" That student returns the greeting and shares "news" in one or two sentences (or responds "No news today.").

3. The second student turns to the third, and the process is repeated around the circle until everyone has been greeted.

Example:

1. Taisha is first and turns to Jill. "Good morning, Jill. What's the news?"

2. Jill responds, "Good morning, Taisha. The news is that my grandma is coming to visit this weekend."

3. Jill then turns to Ricardo and says, "Good morning, Ricardo. What's the news?"

4. Ricardo greets Jill and shares his "news."

5. The process is repeated around the circle.

What's the News?

Grades K–8

About the Author

Melissa Correa-Connolly has been an elementary and middle school educator for many years. She has been a classroom teacher, a bilingual teacher, a special education teacher, and an academic counselor. She's worked for Northeast Foundation for Children for over ten years as a certified *Responsive Classroom* consulting teacher. She also leads workshops for K–8 teachers on teaching second language learners.

Melissa currently lives in Kissimmee, Florida, where she works as a behavior specialist for the Osceola County Schools. She makes her way into classrooms whenever possible to do Morning Meeting greetings and activities with children.

Illustrators at Work

This book was illustrated by a group of children, ages 7–13.
Here they are seen working on their drawings. We're deeply grateful
for the work they did to make the pages of this book come alive.

About the *Responsive Classroom*® Approach

This book grew out of the work of Northeast Foundation for Children (NEFC) and an approach to teaching known as the *Responsive Classroom* approach. Developed by classroom teachers, this approach consists of highly practical strategies for integrating social and academic learning throughout the school day.

Seven beliefs underlie this approach:

1. The social curriculum is as important as the academic curriculum.

2. How children learn is as important as what they learn: Process and content go hand in hand.

3. The greatest cognitive growth occurs through social interaction.

4. There is a specific set of social skills that children need to learn and practice in order to be successful academically and socially: cooperation, assertion, responsibility, empathy, and self-control.

5. Knowing the children we teach—individually, culturally, and developmentally—is as important as knowing the content we teach.

6. Knowing the families of the children we teach and encouraging their participation is as important as knowing the children we teach.

7. How we, the adults at school, work together to accomplish our shared mission is as important as our individual competence: Lasting change begins with the adult community.

More information and guidance on the
***Responsive Classroom* approach are available through:**

Publications and Resources

- Books, videos, and audios for K–8 educators
- Website with articles and other information: www.responsiveclassroom.org
- Free quarterly newsletter for educators

Professional Development Opportunities

- One-day and weeklong workshops for teachers
- Classroom consultations and other services at individual schools and school districts
- Multi-faceted professional development for administrators and all staff at schools wishing to implement the *Responsive Classroom* approach school-wide

For details, contact:

RESPONSIVE CLASSROOM

Northeast Foundation for Children

800-360-6332

www.responsiveclassroom.org

**About the
*Responsive
Classroom*®
Approach**

Practices at the core of the Responsive Classroom® *approach*

The Morning Meeting Book
By Roxann Kriete with contributions by Lynn Bechtel
For K–8 teachers (2002) 218 pages $19.95

Use Morning Meeting in your classroom to build community, increase students' investment in learning, and improve academic and social skills. Features:

■ *Step-by-step guidelines for holding Morning Meeting* ■ *A chapter on Morning Meeting in middle schools* ■ *45 greetings and 66 group activities* ■ *Frequently asked questions and answers*

The First Six Weeks of School
By Paula Denton and Roxann Kriete
For K–6 teachers (2000) 224 pages $19.95

Structure the first weeks of school to lay the groundwork for a productive year of learning. Includes:

■ *Guidelines for the first six weeks, including daily plans for the first three weeks for grades K–2, grades 3–4, and grades 5–6* ■ *Ideas for building community, teaching routines, introducing engaging curriculum, fostering autonomy* ■ *Games, activities, greetings, songs, read-alouds, and resources especially useful during the early weeks of school*

Classroom Spaces That Work
By Marlynn K. Clayton with Mary Beth Forton
For K–6 teachers (2001) 184 pages $19.95

Create a physical environment that is welcoming, well suited to the needs of students and teachers, and conducive to social and academic excellence. Features:

■ *Practical ideas for arranging furniture* ■ *Suggestions for selecting and organizing materials* ■ *Ideas for creating displays* ■ *Guidelines for setting up a meeting area* ■ *Tips for making the space healthy*

Rules in School
By Kathryn Brady, Mary Beth Forton, Deborah Porter, and Chip Wood
For K–8 teachers (2003) 268 pages $19.95

Establish a calm, safe learning environment and teach children self-discipline with this approach to classroom rules. Includes:

■ *Guidelines for creating rules with students based on their hopes and dreams for school* ■ *Steps in modeling and role playing the rules* ■ *How to reinforce the rules through language* ■ *Guidelines for using logical consequences when rules are broken* ■ *Suggestions for teaching children to live by the rules outside the classroom*

Strategies for Teachers Series